THE KURDS OF IRAQ

THE KURDS OF IRAQ

Tragedy and Hope

♦

by

MICHAEL M. GUNTER

St. Martin's Press
New York

First published in the United States of America 1992
Printed in the United States of America

ISBN 0-312-09084-6
ISBN 0-312-09668-2 (pbk.)

Library of Congress Cataloging-in-Publication Data

Gunter, Michael M.
The Kurds in Iraq / Michael M. Gunter.
          p. cm.
     Includes bibliographical references and index.
     ISBN 0-312-09084-6   ISBN 0-312-09668-2 (pbk.)
     1. Kurds—Iraq, Northern—Politics and government. 2. Kurds-
     -Civil rights—Iraq, Northern. 3. Iraq—Politics and government.
     4. Iraq—Ethnic relations. I. Title.
DS70.8.K8G86 1992
956.7'0049159—dc20   92-30309
                                                              CIP

Dedicated to my mother
Larissa Kostenko Gunter

Contents

Acknowledgments

I first became interested in the Middle East when I spent a year as a Senior Fulbright Lecturer in International Relations at the Middle East Technical University in Ankara, Turkey, during the 1978-79 academic year. These were trying times, but I will never forget the many different people and things I saw and did, as I travelled through the area. Now more than a decade later I have the opportunity to write an objective analysis that I hope will shed some light on one particular political problem in the region.

In writing this book and throughout much of my career, I have had the benefit of advice from a number of good and wise friends, including Boleslaw Boczek, Adda Bozeman, Richard Cooper, Steve Khleif, Heath Lowry, Sanford Silverburg, and Michael Turner, among numerous others. Ambassador William Eagleton, Jr., and Mehrdad Izady, in particular, were generous with their time, advice, and information in the writing of this book. Nader Entessar, Edmund Ghareeb, and Robert Olson also read the text and offered their advice. Paul Stephenson, the chairman of the Department of Political Science at Tennessee Technological University, where I have taught for the past twenty years, arranged for me to receive a certain amount of released time, which greatly aided me in the writing of this book. Over the years too I have owed a special debt of gratitude to Eloise Ramsey Hitchcock of the Tennessee Technological University Library for the help she has given me.

Although I have used numerous other libraries over the years, I would like to mention specifically the Columbia University Libraries in New York, New York; the Vanderbilt University Library in Nashville, Tennessee; and the Kurdish Library and its understanding director, Vera Beaudin Saeedpour, in Brooklyn, New York. Samande Siaband (Mehrdad Izady) allowed me to use the excellent map he drew of Central Kurdistan.

Names and terms from Kurdish, Arabic, Farsi, and Turkish appear in this study. To use a consistent transliteration system for them might have resulted in making some appear needlessly awkward or virtually unrecognizable. Therefore, I have used spellings that seemed most natural to me, an English-speaking reader. Similarly, only Kurdish words in the text not commonly used in English have been italicized. To simplify the text, I also have omitted certain diacritical marks. Although the purist might object, such procedures have not affected the meanings of these terms.

In addition, I would like to make it clear that what follows is preeminently a *political* analysis. Where they have impinged upon this domain, of course, I have considered economic, sociological, and religious factors, but I will leave their exposition to others more qualified. Finally, I want to thank Simon Winder of St. Martin's Press who has helped and encouraged me. The final result, however, is mine.

Michael M. Gunter
July 1992

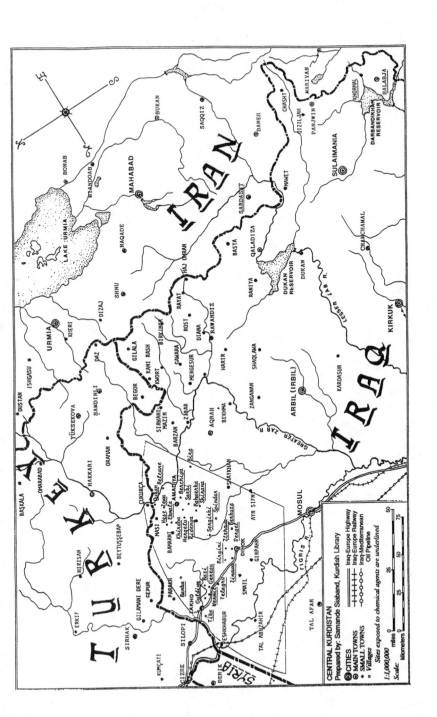

CENTRAL KURDISTAN
Prepared by: Samande Siaband, Kurdish Library

◎ CITIES   ━━━━ Iraq-Europe Highway
◉ MAIN TOWNS   ┼┼┼┼┼ Iraq-Europe Railway
• SMALL TOWNS   ○○○○○ Iraq-Mediterranean
· Villages   Oil Pipeline

Sites exposed to chemical agents are underlined

Scale: 1:1,000,000

miles 0   25   50   75
kilometers 0   25   50   75

1

Background

The Kurds in Iraq[1] have been in an almost constant state of revolt ever since Britain artificially created that state out of the former Ottoman vilayets of Mosul, Baghdad, and Basra following World War I. There are three major reasons for this situation.

First, the Kurds in Iraq long constituted a greater proportion of the population than they did in any other country they inhabited.[2] Accordingly, despite their smaller absolute numbers, they represented a larger critical mass in Iraq than elsewhere, a situation that enabled them to play a more important role there than they did in Turkey and Iran. Second, as an artificial, new state, Iraq had less legitimacy as a political entity than Turkey and Iran, two states that had existed in one form or another for many centuries despite their large Kurdish minorities. Thus, discontent and rebellion came easier for the Iraqi Kurds. Indeed, since the creation of Iraq, it had been understood that they were to negotiate their future position, a right that the Kurds in other states did not have. And third, Iraq was further divided by a Sunni-Shiite Muslim division not present in Turkey or Iran. This predicament further called into question its future.[3]

For its part, the Iraqi government has always feared the possibility of Kurdish separatism. Kurdish secession would not only deplete the Iraqi population; it would also set a precedent that the Shiites, some 55 percent of the population, might follow and thus threaten the very future of the Iraqi state. What is more, since approximately two-thirds of the oil production and reserves, as well as much of the fertile land, were located in the Kurdish area, the government felt that Kurdish secession would strike at the economic heart of the state. Thus were sown the seeds of a seemingly irreconcilable struggle between Iraq and its Kurdish minority.

Number 12 of U.S. President Woodrow Wilson's Fourteen Points had declared that the non-Turkish minorities of the Ottoman Empire should be granted the right of "autonomous development." In addition, the Treaty of Sevres (1920) had provided for "local autonomy for the predominantly Kurdish areas" (Article 62) and in Article 64 even looked forward to the possibility that "the Kurdish peoples" might be granted "independence from Turkey."

The definitive Treaty of Lausanne (1923), however, which made no mention of the Kurds, overruled both of these documents. What is more, the British, who held Iraq as a mandate from the League of Nations, already had decided to attach the largely Kurdish vilayet of Mosul to Iraq because of its vast oil resources.[4] It was thought that this was the only way Iraq could be made viable.

Nevertheless, both the British and the Iraqi government issued a number of statements that theoretically recognized and guaranteed Kurdish rights. On December 24, 1922, for example, an Anglo-Iraqi Joint Declaration to the Council of the League of Nations clearly recognized the right of the Iraqi Kurds to some type of autonomy.

> His Britannic Majesty's Government and the Government of Iraq recognize the right of the Kurds who live within the frontiers of Iraq to establish a Government within those frontiers. Our two Governments hope that the various Kurdish groups will reach some mutual agreement as quickly as possible as to the form they wish this Government to take and as to the boundaries within which they wish to extend its authority. These groups will send responsible delegates to negotiate their future economic and political relations with His Majesty's Government and the Iraqi Government.[5]

Interestingly, it was not until 1926 that the Council of the League of Nations formally recognized the incorporation of Mosul into Iraq; before then Turkey had continued to claim the area.[6] At that time, however, the International Commission of Inquiry established by the Council required that "the desire of the Kurds that the administrators, magistrates and teachers in their country be drawn from their own ranks, and adopt Kurdish as the official language in all their activities, will be taken into account."[7] Although Baghdad issued a "Local Languages Law," these pledges to the Kurds were not included in the Anglo-Iraqi Treaty of 1930, which granted Iraq its independence in 1932.

On the other hand, Stephen H. Longrigg, an authority on Iraqi history, has argued that "in adopting a hesitant attitude to Kurdish claims, the Iraq Government was not always unreasonable. These claims were at times frankly separatist. . . . The fear existed, in addition, that privileges granted to the Kurds would be demanded immediately by the Shi'is of the Euphrates."[8] Longrigg therefore concluded that, as a result, "the

Kurds . . . represented a profoundly unsatisfactory and even a menacing element in the national life [of Iraq]."[9]

From the very beginning, important Kurdish elements opposed the cavalier manner in which they were treated. It also should be noted, however, that other Kurdish groups supported the British and later, Baghdad. Analogous divisions continued into the 1990s, as will be analyzed later.

As the British prepared to accept the League's mandate for Iraq, they invited a local Kurdish leader, Shaikh Mahmud Barzinji of Sulaymaniya, to act as their governor there in 1919. Despite his inability to overcome the divisions among the Kurds, Shaikh Mahmud almost immediately proclaimed himself "King of Kurdistan," revolted against British rule, and began secret dealings with the Turks. In a precursor to subsequent defeats at the hands of the Iraqi government in Baghdad, the British Royal Air Force (RAF) successfully bombed the shaikh's forces, putting down several of his uprisings during the 1920s.

Meanwhile, the only serious opposition to the British institution of the Hashemite monarchy in Iraq occurred in the Kurdish regions. Most of the negative votes came from Kirkuk, while Sulaymaniya did not even participate in the referendum that approved it. Indeed Shaikh Mahmud styled himself "King of Kurdistan" in part to show his opposition to Faisal becoming king of Iraq. It would be a mistake, however, to see the activities of the shaikh as exercises of Kurdish nationalism. At the height of his appeal, he never exceeded the primordial bounds of tribalism.

Genuine Kurdish nationalist feeling did manifest itself in September 1930, however, when strikes and demonstrations broke out in Sulaymaniya. For perhaps the first time it appeared that the Kurdish leadership was moving from the religious and tribal countryside to the cities and their emerging middle classes.

If so, the change was only partial. With the final defeat of Shaikh Mahmud in the spring of 1931,[10] Mulla Mustafa Barzani began to emerge as the leader almost synonymous with the Kurdish movement in Iraq. Despite his eventual wide appeal, however, Barzani remained ultimately a traditional, tribal leader. This situation would prove to be the ultimate weakness of the Kurdish national movement in Iraq.

◆ ◆ ◆

2

Mulla Mustafa Barzani and the Kurdish Movement before 1975

ORIGINS

Early information about the Barzani tribe is obscure and contradictory, although most sources agree that it was only established early in the nineteenth century by a certain Taj ad-Din (Ya'qub or Abd al-Rahman). According to one version Taj ad-Din (an Arabic honorific that means "Crown of Religion") moved from the village of Bahrka just north of Arbil, drove out the earlier Christian and Jewish residents, and settled in a virtually inaccessible part of mountainous, northeastern Iraq on the opposite, northern bank of the Great Zab River.[1] The new home was called "Bar Zan," which in Kurdish meant "migration place." Other versions, however, indicate that the village of Barzan was already in existence when Taj ad-Din first arrived.

All agree that Taj ad-Din became a shaikh (religious leader) when he was initiated into the Naqshbandi Sufi order by the noted mystic saint Maulana Khalid (died 1826), or one of the saint's followers. It has been argued that the "Kurds were more prone than Arabs to Sufism because of its consonance with their pre-Islamic beliefs."[2] Be that as it may—and although mystical, religious orders have been declining among the Kurds since the 1930s—it is clear that the Barzani family owes a great deal of its authority, past and present, to the position it holds over the adherents of the Naqshbandi order.

In addition, of course, as Mark Sykes, the noted authority on the Middle East, observed early in the twentieth century, the Barzanis were a tribe "famous for its fighting qualities."[3] At first glance this was perhaps strange because, when Sykes wrote, the Barzanis numbered only

750 families compared to their tribal enemies the Zibaris (1,000) and the Herkis (3,000). Even by 1945, the adherents of the Shaikh of Barzan numbered only perhaps 1,800 families, or 9,000 people. It was ironic that such a small, primitive, feudal tribe would produce the most famous Kurdish nationalist of the twentieth century and become the leader of Kurdish nationalism.

Shaikh Taj ad-Din was succeeded by his son, or possibly younger brother, Abd al-Salam I (Ishaq), who may have been hanged by the Turks at Mosul when he journeyed there to negotiate a settlement after leading a revolt. His son Muhammad, the new shaikh, was famous for his religious mysticism, a characteristic that eventually may have helped cost him his life. Apparently, as an old man, Muhammad spoke at length about the Mahdi and his ability to fly. In 1908 some of Muhammad's fanatical followers threw him to his death out an upper window of his home to test whether he was indeed the Mahdi and would fly. Other versions state, however, that it was Abd al-Salam I who was thus dispatched by his followers when he refused to lead them against the sultan, while Muhammad died of natural causes.

Be that as it may, Muhammad had at least four sons: Abd al- Salam II, Ahmad (born c. 1884), Mulla Mustafa (born c. 1904), and Siddiq. The eldest, Shaikh Abd al-Salam II, succeeded to the religious leadership of the Barzanis and, like his father, grandfather, and younger brother Ahmad, was at times accused of religious heresy. After he resisted some new laws imposed by the Young Turk regime and apparently intrigued with the Russians, he was hanged in Mosul in 1914 or, according to another version, 1916.

SHAIKH AHMAD

The new shaikh, Ahmad, was to earn a reputation for eccentricity and mental imbalance greater than his predecessors. In 1927, for example, he in effect developed a new sect that exalted his person to a degree close to divinity. The tribal reaction that followed resulted in the death of his younger brother, Siddiq. Government intervention followed. Ahmad's claims dissipated, but his influence remained. The government may have encouraged these allegations against Ahmad because it regarded the Barzanis as dangerous opponents. A policy of divide and rule toward the Kurds would be useful.

Be that as it may, in July 1931 Shaikh Ahmad further tested his followers by imposing "Christianity" and ordering them to eat pork. A more orthodox member of the Naqshbandi order, Shaikh Rashid of Baradost, declared a holy war against the Barzanis but was soundly beaten by Ahmad's younger brother, Mulla Mustafa, who now entered the scene. The younger Barzani also beat off an Iraqi army advance, forcing the RAF to intervene. Partially chastened, Shaikh Ahmad reverted to a more orthodox Islamic doctrine.

When the Barzanis opposed a plan to settle Assyrians in their tribal area and refused to pay taxes to the new Iraqi government in the spring of 1932, the authorities again moved against them. Although Mulla Mustafa enjoyed some early successes, RAF bombing eventually forced him and Ahmad over the Turkish border where they surrendered to the Turks on June 22, 1932. Ahmad was held in Istanbul and latter Edirne.

Shortly afterward, the Barzani brothers were returned to Iraq. They were arrested and exiled first to Nasiriya in southern Iraq and then Sulaymaniya in the north. This latter choice was probably a mistake on the part of the government; Sulaymaniya was the center of budding Kurdish national awareness, a city "dear to all Kurds for its well laid out and exemplarily clean streets, its climate which is brisk, even in summer, its industrious population, its lively shops and [later] for the young people who flock to its university."[4] It was here that young Mulla Mustafa undoubtedly began to stretch his limited, tribal horizons and reach instead for a beginning appreciation of Kurdish nationalism.

MULLA MUSTAFA

As indicated, young Mulla Mustafa's early years were scarred by violence and death. His father was apparently killed by religious fanatics in 1908 and his eldest brother was hanged by the Ottoman government in 1914. He himself was imprisoned by the Ottomans with his mother for nine months when he was not yet two years old. Undoubtedly these seminal events influenced his later views toward "legitimate" authority.

The boy received six years of primary education from private tutors in Barzan and then studied theology there for four more years.[5] During his exile in Sulaymaniya during the 1930s, he furthered his religious studies to the extent that he learned to recite and explain all the Koranic verses and to quote and interpret the sayings of the Prophet.

Accordingly, some have concluded that "he was awarded the religious title Mulla."[6] Most observers state, however, that the name was not of religious significance. Dana Adams Schmidt, a correspondent for the New York Times who visited and befriended Barzani in the 1960s, still declared, after detailing the Kurdish leader's religious upbringing, that Barzani "was named 'Mullah,' it should be noted, not for any religious reason but after a maternal uncle."[7] Whether or not such a namesake ever existed, a confidential report by the U.S. Central Intelligence Agency (CIA) did agree: "It should be noted that in this case, Mullah is a proper name and not a title."[8]

Barzani originally may have received the name because of his religious studies; given the later development of his career as a secular leader, however, the name lost its religious connotation and simply began to imply that he was well educated or simply literate. His elder brother, Shaikh Ahmad, played the religious role in the family, while Mulla Mustafa rose to be the greatest Kurdish secular and national leader of the twentieth century.

In the late 1920s, Barzani married the first of three wives. The first two marriages resulted in three sons—Ubaidallah (born c. 1927), Loqman, and Idris—and a daughter. For apparent political reasons he also later married the daughter of Mahmoud Agha, the leader of his hereditary enemy, the Zibari tribe. This third wife, who later was to exercise considerable personal influence in the Kurdish movement, bore him at least four more sons, Massoud (born c. 1945), Sabir (c. 1946), Nahad (born in the 1950s), and another after 1960. When he finally died in 1979, however, "Barzani was reported to have 10 children and a wife who has been living in [Karaj near] Teheran."[9]

Barzani was described by those who knew him as having "an imposing figure,"[10] "a man of exceptionally powerful build,"[11] and "huskily built with a bull neck that went square into his shoulders. His complexion was swarthy and his black hair was cropped short. By far his most conspicuous features were deep brown eyes."[12] Of medium height, Barzani wore the gray and white dress and red and white turban of his tribe with a double cartridge belt around his waist. U.S. Ambassador William Eagleton, Jr., wrote that Barzani "quickly grasped the essence of a situation and exercised diplomatic and military cunning in achieving his objective."[13] He added, however, that "less commendable characteristics were Mulla Mustafa's egotism, opportunism, shortsightedness, and intractability."

Dana Adams Schmidt further observed that "food at General Barzani's headquarters is likely to be worse than in any village along the way. He does not pamper himself or those around him."[14] He was "a man who maintained dignity and calm in all circumstances. He might be angered. But he never raged. He laughed, but not uproariously. . . . Although he assumed . . . democratic attitudes, Barzani always maintained . . . an aristocratic reserve." Schmidt added that "while he could be extremely charming and affable, he could also at times verge on rudeness" and that Barzani's "remarks often had a cryptic, delphic quality. . . . He liked to convey his ideas by telling stories."

During the 1960s, the Iraqi government unflatteringly characterized Barzani in the following manner: "Mulla began as a freebooter. . . . Truly speaking, the whole problem centres round one man. . . . He survives in his leadership only as long as the killing continues."[15]

Escape to Barzan

In the fall of 1943, Mulla Mustafa ended his exile in Sulaymaniya and escaped to Barzan where he reestablished his position at the expense of rival Kurdish tribes and the Iraqi government. In so doing he was helped by Heva (Hope), a liberal, nationalist party of urban intellectuals established in 1941. For the first time in his career, Barzani began to rise above his mere tribal origins and assume a role as a Kurdish spokesman.

Since World War II was still raging and the British were hard put to maintain their position in Iraq, they advised Baghdad to negotiate with the rebelling Kurds. Prime Minister Nuri Said, who may have been of partial Kurdish ancestry, was predisposed to do so. He accordingly sent Majid Mustafa, who was a Kurd as well as a successful provincial governor, as minister without portfolio to meet with Barzani.

The main Kurdish demands were that a Kurdish province consisting of the districts of Kirkuk, Sulaymaniya, Arbil, Dohuk, and Khanaqin be given cultural, economic, and agricultural autonomy, and all internal matters, except those concerning the army and the gendarmerie, be placed under a special minister for Kurdish affairs in the Iraqi Cabinet. Among other things, this meant that Kurdish would actually be taught in the schools as it supposedly had been since 1932, and recognized as an official language. In addition, a Kurdish assistant minister would be appointed to each ministry.[16]

At first the Iraqi government seemed prepared to meet some of these demands and Barzani even accompanied Majid Mustafa to Baghdad. Shaikh Ahmad was released in early 1944 and allowed to return to Barzan, where he resumed his religious leadership. But in time a majority of the government found the demands excessive and feared that they would lead to still more, including separatist tendencies. Nuri Said was forced to resign in June 1944; Majid Mustafa was dismissed, and soon new fighting broke out.

By now Barzani had built a considerable military force, and at first they experienced some major successes. In time, however, bombing raids and government use of Kurdish tribes such as the Zibaris as loyalist troops forced Barzani to withdraw across the Iranian frontier with several thousand members of his tribe. The logistics of moving such a large group under hostile conditions were considerable, and their successful conclusion added to Barzani's reputation.

The Mahabad Republic

The story of the only Kurdish state in the twentieth century has been told elsewhere.[17] Here it should only be noted that a temporary vacuum of authority along the Iraqi-Iranian frontier, due to the occupation of Iran by the Soviet Union and Britain during World War II, had allowed Qazi Muhammad, an Iranian Kurdish nationalist and intellectual who enjoyed Soviet backing, to declare independence in January 1946. Although Barzani was at first ironically looked upon as a "British agent" by the Soviets advising the Iranian Kurds, his arrival proved a godsend and he eventually became an important force in—some say the commanding general of—the short-lived republic.

With the destruction of this state late in 1946, the Barzani tribe withdrew to the mountainous border region. Finally, with some of his best fighters, Barzani made an epic retreat to the Soviet Union against great odds. Later Barzani recalled that "we marched for fifty-two days. In the high mountain passes the late spring snow was six to twelve feet deep. We fought nine encounters, lost four killed and had seven wounded."[18] Near the end they passed through two Iranian battalions without being detected. The Barzanis entered the Soviet Union in the middle of June 1947 at a point south of the Soviet frontier post at Sarachlu.

The retreat was necessary because leaders in Baghdad were prepared to execute Barzani if he fell into their hands. Indeed, four of his officers were hanged on June 29, 1947, while Shaikh Ahmad was imprisoned once more, this time for more than a decade.[19]

The Soviet Union

When Barzani first arrived in the Soviet Union, he was received with considerable caution, "but at least they did not send us back to Iraq."[20] He spent some months in Baku and then went to Tashkent, while his men were dispersed throughout the country. When they wanted to go to the market or elsewhere, they had to ask permission and have a chaperon go with them.

In time, the Barzanis were given more freedom to move about. Barzani himself learned Russian and also studied economics, geography, and science. Occasionally he would make radio broadcasts back to Iraq from Erevan in Soviet Armenia. During the summer, he was allowed to visit his men. Most were working in factories, while some studied in institutions of higher learning or worked on farms. Approximately eighty were married to Soviet citizens. In 1954 Barzani and his two main associates of that time, Assad Hoshewi and Mir Haj, were given apartments in Moscow. Barzani attended the Academy of Languages there.

Although he became known as the "Red Mulla" in the West, Barzani maintained that "we are Moslems and good Moslems cannot be Communists," adding that "I spent twelve years in Russia and I did not become a Communist." His subsequent career proved these protestations.

Return to Iraq

On July 14, 1958, General Abdul Karim Kassem overthrew the Hashemite monarchy in a bloody coup. Barzani was in Prague enjoying a holiday. He immediately telegraphed for permission to return, and it was granted. His route home led through Cairo where he was received by President Gamal Abdul Nasser, but their talks were not substantive.[21]

When he first returned to Baghdad on October 6, 1958, Barzani was welcomed by Kassem and given the mansion the assassinated Nuri Said had lived in, as well as a limousine. Kassem also legalized Barzani's Kurdish Democratic Party (KDP) and permitted the publication of fourteen Kurdish journals, including *Khebat* (*Struggle*) and *Kurdistan,* both organs of the KDP, as well *Zhin* (*Life*), *Hetaw* (*Sun*), and *Azadi* (*Liberty*), which was the organ of the Kurdish Section of the Iraqi Communist Party (ICP). Article 23 of the new provisional constitution (July 27, 1958) gave the Kurds a recognition they had never before received in any other state when it declared: "The Kurds and the Arabs are partners within this nation. The Constitution guarantees their rights within the framework of the Iraqi Republic."

Whatever else Barzani requested seemed to be granted—especially arms to fight against Kassem's numerous, reactionary enemies and pro-Nasser opponents. When the Second Iraqi Army Division stationed in Mosul under Colonel Abd al-Wahhab al- Shawwaf revolted on March 8, 1959, and announced its intentions of taking Baghdad, for example, Kassem used Barzani's Kurds and the communists to defeat and kill Shawwaf. In so doing, the communists committed numerous atrocities, which gave them an unfavorable reputation.

Gradually, however, Kassem and Barzani drifted apart as it became clear to both of them that their ultimate intentions were mutually incompatible. In October 1960 Barzani accepted an invitation to attend the annual celebration of the Bolshevik revolution in Moscow. He did not return to Iraq until March 1961, although he remained the effective leader of the Barzanis. By that time the Barzanis had already regained their position in northern Iraq at the expense of some of their traditional tribal enemies.

In July 1961 Barzani presented Kassem a petition that demanded full Kurdish autonomy.[22] According to this document, Kurdish was to become the official language of the Kurdish autonomous region. The police and army units stationed in the Kurdish region were to be entirely Kurdish. The Kurdish autonomous government was to control education, health services, communications, and municipal and rural affairs. A large share of the oil revenues garnered from the Kurdish region was to be spent there. Foreign affairs, defense, and national financial policy were to be the prerogative of Baghdad, but the vice-premier, assistant chief of staff, and all the assistant ministers of the ministries were to be Kurds. Finally Kurdish army units could be used outside the autonomous region only with the consent of its leaders, except in cases of external threats to Iraq. Fearing that to acquiesce to these provisions would be to invite the dismemberment of Iraq, Kassem refused.

Later Baghdad explained its position in some detail[23]: "The concessions which the Kurds of Iraq under Mulla Mustafa's leadership demand are out of proportion with their number in this country, the area of land inhabited by them or the contribution made by them as a community to the national output." The government declared that "the demand for the creation of a separate armed force" constituted "unmistakable pointers to something deeper, sinister and . . . has absolutely no parallel in world history." As for the oil, "natural resources are nowhere in the world considered the private property of the small section of population inhabiting the site of their discovery or exploitation." Comparing its policy to Turkey and Iran, Baghdad also argued that "Iraq is the only country that acknowledges their [the Kurds'] separate identity ungrudgingly. This country does not frown upon the use by them of their own dress or language." Sarcastically, however, the government concluded: "We know how Iraq has been rewarded for this fond indulgence!"

Renewed Hostilities

Barzani's rise to prominence after his return in 1958 is not easy to explain fully. As late as 1957, no less an astute observer of affairs than C.

J. Edmonds, who had been a British Political Officer in Iraq during the 1920s and who has written a number of useful analyses of the Iraqi Kurds, mentioned Barzani only in passing as a "fugitive rebel from Iraq,"[24] and concluded that "with every year that passes any concerted armed revolt becomes more improbable." Two years later, although now realizing that "the event which perhaps more than any other has caught the popular imagination is the return of Mulla Mustafa,"[25] Edmonds could only argue that "it is difficult to explain this rapid build-up into a national all-Iraqi figure . . . otherwise than as the work of a well-organized chain of communist propagandists long established throughout Iraq."

Although the communists undoubtedly had helped, Kassem himself unwittingly facilitated matters even more by allowing Barzani to return in the first place and then hailing him as a hero. Barzani's rise would still not have been possible, however, if he himself had not (1) led the revolt in 1945 against both the old imperialist power, Britain, and the new royal one of Iraq, (2) carried out the organized retreat to Mahabad and then served as that ephemeral Kurdish state's military leader, and finally (3) refused to submit to the oppressive victors but instead miraculously escaped to exile in the Soviet Union from where he remained in touch with his people in Iraq through occasional radio broadcasts.

What is more, Kurdish national feeling had become more developed with the spread of modernity and westernization. Although some Kurdish tribes still favored the government, many young Kurds from tribes previously opposed to the Barzanis now supported them, as did a number of Kurdish soldiers in the Iraqi army.

Thus buoyed, Barzani assembled as many as 7,000 armed combatants, started to occupy strategic points, and expelled the government police and small garrisons. Full-scale hostilities began when the government bombed Barzan in September 1961. The cruel and indiscriminate bombing of Kurdish villages, in which the majority of casualties were women, children, and old people, brought still more supporters to Barzani.

Despite their numerical superiority in troops and equipment, the governments in Baghdad were weak until the end of the 1960s. Barzani successfully fought a classic guerrilla war by refusing to defend fixed positions. Even Barzan was abandoned, as Barzani correctly realized that he was winning as long as he continued to exist. Knowing virtually every inch of the terrain, the Kurdish guerrillas, or peshmergas (those who are willing to face death for their cause), never allowed themselves to be surrounded, always managing to slip away before the government forces could entrap them.

The Baath Party[26] overthrew Kassem on February 8, 1963. The party fell from power nine months later, but resumed power in July 1968. Throughout the 1960s, conflict between the government and the Kurds (broken by occasional cease-fires and negotiations) raged. Although outnumbered and outgunned, Barzani's peshmergas gave a good account of themselves, withstanding major offensives in June 1963, May 1966, and again at the end of 1968. Indeed, in late May 1966 the Kurds won such a spectacular victory near Mt. Hindarin, northeast of Rawanduz, that the civilian prime minister, Abdul Rahman al-Bazzaz, offered the "29 June Declaration" that specifically recognized Kurdish national rights.[27] Although Barzani accepted it as a basis for negotiations, the Iraqi military would not and forced al-Bazzaz to resign.

The March 1970 Manifesto

Aware that the inability to solve the Kurdish problem was a major reason for the fall of several Iraqi regimes including its own in the 1960s and following yet another bloody but indecisive military campaign, the Baath Party, under President Ahmad Hassan al-Bakr and Vice-President Saddam Hussein, finally sent Aziz Sharif, a former communist, to begin negotiations with Barzani. Michel Aflaq, one of the two founders of the Baath Party, added his authority to the attempt to reach a peaceful settlement based on "the Kurds' right to have a sort of autonomy."[28] At the end Saddam Hussein himself, who was apparently the main Baathist sponsor of the Manifesto, journeyed north to meet with Barzani early in March 1970 and assure the Kurds of his government's good intentions. The final result was the famous fifteen articles of the Manifesto of March 11, 1970. Since it was held at the time to be a historic achievement, has been continually referred to over the years as a background for a settlement by both sides, and was declared the basis of the negotiations that took place after the uprising in 1991, it would be valuable to cite the Manifesto in detail.[29]

(1) The Kurdish language shall, side by side with the Arabic language, be an official language in the areas populated by a majority of Kurds. The Kurdish language shall be the language of instruction in these areas. The Arabic language shall be taught in all schools where teaching is conducted in Kurdish. The Kurdish language shall be taught elsewhere in Iraq as a second language within the limits prescribed by the law.

(2) It has been one of the main concerns of the revolutionary government [Baghdad] to secure participation by our Kurdish brothers in Government and eliminate any discrimination between Kurds and other nationals in regard to

holding public offices including sensitive and important ones as cabinet ministries, army commands, etc. . . .

(3) In view of the backwardness experienced in the past by the Kurdish nationality in the cultural and educational domains, a plan should be worked out . . . in regard to the language and cultural rights of the Kurdish people, . . . reinstating students who were dismissed or had to leave school because of former conditions of violence in the area, . . . building more schools in the Kurdish area, elevating the standards of education and admitting, at a fair rate, Kurdish students to universities and military colleges and granting them scholarships.

(4) In the administrative units populated by a Kurdish majority, government officials shall be appointed from among Kurds or persons well versed in the Kurdish language as long as these are available. The principal Government functionaries—governor, district officer (Qaimuqam), director of police, director of security, etc.—shall be drawn from among the Kurds. . . .

(5) The Government recognizes the right of the Kurdish people to set up student, youth, women and teacher's organizations of their own. These organizations shall be affiliated in the national counterparts in Iraq.

(6) . . . Workers, government functionaries and employees, both civilian and military [who fought on the Kurdish side during the hostilities], shall go back to service. . . .

(7) (a) A committee of specialists shall be formed to speed up the uplift of the Kurdish area in all respects and provide indemnities for the affliction of the past number of years, side by side with drawing up an adequate budget for all of this. The committee in question shall be attached to the Ministry of Northern Affairs. (b) The economic plan shall be drawn up in such a way as to ensure equal development for various parts of Iraq, with due attention to the backward conditions of the Kurdish area. (c) Pension salaries shall be made available to the families of members of the Kurdish armed movement who met with martyrdom in the regrettable hostilities as well as to those rendered incapacitated or disfigured. . . . (d) Speedy action shall be taken to bring relief to aggrieved and needy persons. . . .

(8) The inhabitants of Arab and Kurdish villages shall be repatriated to their places of habitation. As to villagers whose villages lie in areas requisitioned by the Government for public utility purposes . . . they shall be settled in neighbouring districts and shall be compensated for whatever loss they might have incurred as a result.

(9) Steps shall be taken to speed up the implementation of the Agrarian Reform Law in the Kurdish area and have the Law amended in such a way as to ensure the liquidation of all feudalistic relationship[s], handing out appropriate plots of land to all peasants and waiving for them agricultural tax arrears for the duration of the regrettable hostilities.

(10) It has been agreed to amend the Interim Constitution as follows: (a) The people of Iraq are composed of two principal nationalities: the Arab nationality and the Kurdish nationality. This Constitution recognizes the national rights of the Kurdish people and the rights of all nationalities within

the framework of the Iraqi unity. (b) The following paragraph shall be added to Article (4) of the Constitution: "The Kurdish language shall be, beside the Arabic language, an official language in the Kurdish area. (c) This all shall be confirmed in the Permanent Constitution.

(11) The broadcasting station and the heavy arms shall be given back to the Government—this being tied up to the implementation of the final stages of the agreement.

(12) One of the Vice-Presidents of the Republic shall be a Kurd.

(13) The Governorates Law shall be amended in a way conforming with the contents of this Manifesto.

(14) Following the issuance of the Manifesto, necessary steps shall be taken in consultation with the High Committee supervising its enforcement to unify the governorates and administrative units populated by a Kurdish majority as shown by the official census to be carried out. The State shall endeavour to develop this administrative unity and deepen and broaden the Kurdish people's process of exercising their national rights as a measure of ensuring self-rule. Pending the realization of administrative unity, Kurdish national affairs shall be coordinated by means of periodical meetings between the High Committee and the governors of the northern area. As self-rule is to be established within the framework of the Republic of Iraq, the exploitation of the natural riches in the area shall obviously be the prerogative of the authorities of the Republic.

(15) The Kurdish people shall contribute to the legislative power in proportion to their ratio of the population of Iraq.

In a preliminary statement, the March 1970 Manifesto even decreed that the Kurdish new year's celebration of *Nawroz*[30] would be a national holiday. Clearly the Manifesto was a generous and apparently sincere attempt on the part of the Iraqi government to meet legitimate Kurdish demands. Why then did it fail to work?

Failure

Although the Manifesto, taken at face value, was a path by which the Kurdish problem could have been solved, lack of mutual trust prevented it from succeeding. Indeed, one now wonders if Baghdad—and for that matter even the Kurds—really wanted to implement it, or whether they were actually just playing for time until what they saw as the next inevitable round of hostilities began. Illustrative of this situation, Ibrahim Ahmad, the former secretary-general of the KDP, once admitted that the definition of Kurdish autonomy would "depend on our strength and that of our enemy."[31]

According to the Kurds, the High Committee mentioned in Articles 7 and 14 of the Manifesto—a joint group consisting of Baathist and Kurdish representatives charged with implementing the agreement—ran into difficulties almost immediately. Specific problems involved the extent of the Kurdish autonomous area established by Articles 4 and 14, and whether the oil-rich area of Kirkuk would be part of it. One Kurdish commentator reproached the government for granting "a mere half of Kurdistan"[32] to the autonomous area, while Barzani accused the Baathists of trying to alter the demographic composition of Kirkuk by moving in Arab settlers.

When the government issued the new, provisional constitution in July 1970, it did not include the amendments concerning "the national rights of the Kurdish people" as promised by Article 10 of the Manifesto. The provisions concerning the Kurdish language in Article 1 were honored only in a very limited manner, while the pledge in Article 8 to halt the policy of "Arabizing" the Kurdish lands was not maintained. Indeed, in September 1971 Baghdad expelled some 40,000 Faili Kurds—who had lived for generations in Baghdad or south of Khanaqin—on the grounds that these Shiite Kurds were really Iranian nationals. Assassination attempts also were made against Barzani's son, Idris, and then Barzani himself; the Baathists were the prime suspects. Saddam Hussein frequently employed such tactics in his rise to power.[33]

According to the Baathists, on the other hand, "the factors endangering the process of the reconstruction of peace . . . [and] constituting a danger to the security of the state and to our future cooperation"[34] were the fault of Barzani's Kurds. The party enumerated thirty-five provisions prescribed by the March Manifesto that they had implemented, including several that the Kurds had claimed had not been effected. These included "amending the Interim Constitution in a way affirming the national presence of the Kurds," "taking legal measures to ensure the recognition of the Kurdish language . . . as an official language," "appointment of Kurdish officials in the administrative units inhabited by a Kurdish majority," and so forth.

In addition, the Baathists tried to explain why six clauses of the Manifesto had not yet been enforced. In regard to the provisions of Article 14, concerning a census to determine the relative Arab and Kurdish population in certain contested areas, for example, the government declared that Barzani had said he was "not prepared to recognize the results of the census if they indicated the presence of an Arab majority in the enumerated areas."

From here the government's indictment went on to list a long litany of Kurdish violations of the March Manifesto. The role Iran was playing in encouraging Barzani was particularly resented. "First and foremost of the questions that have always constituted a gross violation of the simplest fundamentals of national unity and the oneness of the sovereignty of the Iraqi Republic is, perhaps, the external relations connecting your Party with the ruling reaction in Iran."

Baghdad then listed numerous specific examples of this "insult." These included: (1) "the flow of Iranian arms in substantial quantities into the northern area, particularly during the escalation of . . . strife" between Iraq and Iran; (2) "the arrival of heavy . . . weapons to your forces via Iran; and . .. a new broadcasting station" in violation of Article 11 of the Manifesto; (3) "the training of many Peshmergas in Iran on various weapons, particularly heavy arms"; (4) "the communication of military information concerning the Iraqi army by certain elements who assume certain positions with you, and whose connections with Iran are known to you"; (5) "the siding with the Iranian armed forces in certain frontier clashes"; (6) "the circulation of counterfeit Iraqi currency printed by Iranian intelligence with the aim of destroying the Iraqi currency"; and (7) "the exchange of visits between certain members of the leadership of your Party and Iranian officials."

Baghdad continued by listing a huge range of other illegal actions carried out by Barzani and concluded that "if this is the reality of today, we might well wonder what sort of self-rule your Party is really after." The old fear that the ultimate goal of the Kurds was separation was clearly being alluded to.

The End

In March 1974 the Baathists issued an autonomy law that significantly reduced the concessions previously offered Barzani. Renewed fighting broke out later that month and lasted until March of the following year, when Iraq and Iran signed the Algiers Accord. Under this agreement Iran halted its support of Barzani in return for joint usage of the Shatt-al-Arab River and the transfer of some land to Iran.[35] (See Chapter 4.) Without this aid Barzani could not continue the struggle. In the space of a few short months the great Kurdish leader had fallen from the heights of power and respect.

Barzani first went into exile in Karaj, a suburb of Tehran, and then in the United States where he lived in Alexandria, Virginia, a suburb of Washington, D.C. Although forbidden by the terms of his exile from engaging in public, political activities, he still wrote letters to officials, including President Jimmy Carter. He also labored unsuccessfully to learn English and every few weeks visited the Mayo Clinic for treatment of lung cancer, from which he finally died on March 1, 1979. He still spoke rationally about the Kurdish problem two hours before his death. According to one report, his grandson Farhad was at his side.

Barzani was buried at Ushnavia in the Kurdish region of Iran, where a representative of that state placed a wreath on his tomb and praised him as a "warrior."[36] In a loathsome act illustrative of the bitter divisions that still split the Kurdish people, however, his body was exhumed and desecrated in the early 1980s by Iranian Kurds hostile to his memory.

Two of Barzani's sons, Idris and Massoud, eventually were able to carry on his struggle in northern Iraq. His eldest son, Ubaidallah, however, had earlier broken with his father and joined the Baathists, arguing that Barzani "does not want self-rule to be implemented even if he was given Kirkuk and all of its oil. His acceptance of the law [the March Manifesto] will take everything from him, and he wants to remain the absolute ruler."[37]

If this were true—and probably there is some degree of validity to it—the Baathists were to be faulted even more. Fifteen more years of bloodshed would have to pass before the March Manifesto could be used once again as a basis for renewed hope instead of recurring tragedy.

Although Ubaidallah turned against his father, his latent love and respect for him eventually cost Ubaidallah his life.[38] Ubaidallah was serving as a minister of state in the government of Saddam Hussein. During a meeting in the mid-1980s, after Saddam had criticized Mulla Mustafa, Ubaidallah reportedly blurted out that at least he knew who his father was. Ubaidallah's apparent reference was to Saddam's lowly birth. Shortly afterward, Saddam had Barzani's eldest son murdered for the insult.

In conclusion, it is important to recall that Mulla Mustafa Barzani was the greatest Kurdish hero of the twentieth century. His long, colorful career and many improbable successes in battle gave his people a pride they otherwise would have lacked. Born a traditional tribal agha (feudal landlord or tribal chief), Barzani died a legendary Kurdish patriot. Although he was ultimately defeated, his career helped mightily to foster a nascent Kurdish national consciousness in Iraq that continues into the 1990s.

♦ ♦ ♦

3

The Kurdistan Democratic Party (KDP)

Given the tribal and feudal condition of the Kurds, there were no political parties in the modern sense of the word until a group of notable families founded Khoybun (Independence) in Bihamdun, Lebanon, in August 1927. Over the next several years, this organization sought unsuccessfully to promote independence for greater Kurdistan. The failed uprising in the area around Mt. Ararat under General Ihsan Nuri Pasha in 1930 was one example of these efforts.

In Iraq, however, the absence of any Kurdish party led what few intellectuals there were to join the Iraqi Communist Party (ICP), which had been founded in 1935. Over the years the ICP generally took a favorable attitude toward the Kurdish movement. At times, a number of its senior members were of Kurdish origin, and eventually the party maintained a Kurdish Section or Branch. This helps to explain the otherwise incongruent but important role historically played by the ICP in the Iraqi Kurdish movement.[1] In 1943, moreover, a small Kurdish Communist Party, Shoresh (Revolution), was established. In early 1946, however, this group joined the ICP.

The dearth of Kurdish parties began to change in 1941, when the urban intellectuals of Iraqi Kurdistan created the clandestine Heva (Hope) Party as a nationalist organization embracing the political spectrum from left to right.[2] The resultant rivalries, however, prevented Heva from replacing the traditional tribal leadership or winning the allegiances of any significant number of Kurds. As a matter of practicality, therefore, Heva cooperated with Mulla Mustafa Barzani, helping him to escape from detention in Sulaymaniya in 1943 and in his unsuccessful uprising of 1945.

The Soviets meanwhile encouraged the Iranian Kurds of Mahabad—

who, as mentioned in Chapter 2, were to establish a short-lived Kurdish state there—to transform Komala (Committee) into the Kurdistan Democratic Party of Iran (KDPI) under the leadership of Qazi Muhammad in 1945. The following year Shoresh in Iraq sent Hamza Abdullah to Mahabad to discuss what possibilities of cooperation existed. There Abdullah met Barzani and other Iraqi Kurds. After several meetings they agreed to establish a new party in Iraq modeled after Iran's KDP.

The preeminent Kurdish party in Iraqi history, the Iraqi KDP, was thus created in 1946. At least four different political persuasions participated: Heva, Shoresh, Rizgari (Liberation)—a popular front grouping created by the ICP in 1945—and the Iraqi branch of the Iranian KDP. At its first congress on August 16, 1946, Barzani was elected president or chairman, while Abdullah became the secretary-general. Two landlords, Shaikh Latif (son of Shaikh Mahmud of Sulaymaniya) and Shaikh Ziad Aghaz, were chosen as vice presidents. It also was decided to publish a clandestine monthly called *Rizgari*, later changed to *Khebat* (*Struggle*).

The program of the party was vague, speaking of the Kurds' national goals and their desire to live in a state of their own choice. It lacked any progressive social or economic substance due to the dominance held by the traditional, tribal leaders. Given Barzani's long exile in the Soviet Union until 1958 and the quiescent state of Kurdish affairs until that time, in its first ten years the KDP was destined to play only a minor role. Indeed one observer concluded that what had been established "was more of a social and cultural gathering than a well-defined political party."[3]

In those early years, an intraparty struggle developed between supporters of the party's secretary-general, Hamza Abdullah, apparently more of an opportunist than anything else, and Ibrahim Ahmad, who at first headed the Iraqi branch of the Iranian KDP. Born around 1914, Ahmad was a graduate of the Faculty of Law at the University of Baghdad and had published his thesis on Arab-Kurdish relations in 1937. Although he flirted with communism—as did most Kurdish intellectuals in those days—and even spent three years in prison for communist activities in the early 1950s, Ahmad could be best characterized as a leftist Kurdish nationalist. In the 1960s he was described as "a bookish man . . . small and frail with graying temples and a carefully clipped white mustache."[4] When the Le Monde reporter Eric Roulot visited him at his hiding place in a cave near Sulaymaniya, Ahmad "sat in a well-lighted corner surrounded by books ranging from Dostoevski to Harrison Salisbury, from Shakespeare to Harold Laski and Marx and Lenin."[5]

When Ahmad emerged from prison in 1953, he replaced Abdullah, who himself was then in prison for his political activities, as secretary-general. Barzani, however, did not like the new KDP leader, and spoke disparagingly of his "pride and vanity."[6] With Barzani's support, Abdullah replaced Ahmad as secretary-general briefly in 1959. But Abdullah grew too close to the ICP—apparently proposing to transfer various KDP organizations to its control—and later that year he was permanently removed and Ahmad reinstated.

The most important intraparty conflict, however, became the one between the more conservative and traditional, tribal wing of the KDP associated with Barzani and the leftist, intellectual, Marxist wing (the later, so-called KDP Politburo) led by Ahmad and Jalal Talabani, who was to become his son-in-law. The latter group only grudgingly accepted Barzani because they needed his military prowess.

The Barzani wing was also associated with the Northern Kurmanji (Bahdinani)-speaking areas in the mountainous north, while the Ahmad-Talabani group came from the more cultured Southern Kurmanji (Sorani) dialect that prevailed in the Kurdish towns in the south. As Martin van Bruinessen, a leading authority on the Kurds, has noted: "the 'Soran' often find the 'Kurmanji' primitive and fanatical in religious affairs, but they acknowledge their fighting prowess; the 'Kurmanji' often see the 'Soran' as unmanly, unreliable and culturally arrogant."[7] The fact that Barzani and Talabani were also adherents of the two great, rival Sufi orders in Iraqi Kurdistan—the Naqshbandi and Qadiri—possibly provided a further impetus to their rivalry.

During Barzani's sojourn in the Soviet Union, the KDP fell under the control of the Ahmad or KDP Politburo faction. Barzani's return signaled an intense struggle within the party between him, "the man of the tribes" and the "reformist," "town-bred intellectuals." It was with this background that Barzani skeptically replied, concerning the role of the KDP: "What it can do it does. But according to me, there is no party, only the Kurdish people."[8]

The battle intensified in 1964, when Barzani signed a cease- fire accord with Baghdad without even informing the Politburo. Both factions expelled each other, but Barzani won the day by driving the Politburo over the Iranian frontier. This incident apparently led Iran to transfer its support from the Politburo to Barzani, thus enabling him to increase his control over the movement.

Although Talabani rejoined Barzani in 1965, he soon broke away again, branding Barzani "tribal," "feudal," and "reactionary."[9] This intra-Kurdish rivalry—as well as the similar, radical, social ideas they shared—in time led the Talabani-Ahmad faction to develop ties with the Baathists, who, after they regained power in 1968, were also wary of Barzani's ties with Iran and other foreign powers. Accordingly, Talabani made a deal with Baghdad that allowed him to control the Sulaymaniya-Kirkuk region. On a number of occasions, Talabani's guerrillas even fought alongside the government's troops against Barzani, a situation that helped lead to Barzani's famous characterization of Talabani as "an agent for everybody."[10] At this time Ahmad was living in Tehran and then later Baghdad, thus adding further credence to Barzani's accusation.

The split in the Iraqi Kurdish movement was basic and deep. The Ahmad-Talabani group, in cooperation with the Baathists, was challenging Barzani's leadership of the movement and attempting to expand into his northern, mountainous homeland.

Nevertheless, during the fighting of the late 1960s, Barzani's peshmergas grew into more than 20,000 well-equipped fighters, armed with anti-aircraft guns, field guns, antitank weapons, and increasing Iranian support. As a result, the Baathists finally decided to abandon Talabani and negotiate with Barzani. Both Talabani and Ahmad contritely returned to the KDP, which had become Barzani's virtual fiefdom.

The promise of the March 1970 Manifesto, however, was not realized, and, as described earlier, the renewed fighting led to Barzani's final defeat in March 1975. As will be analyzed in full in Chapter 5, two of Barzani's sons, Massoud and Idris, eventually established their control over a new KDP, while Talabani finally institutionalized his beliefs and programs by establishing the Patriotic Union of Kurdistan (PUK) in Damascus in June 1976.

♦ ♦ ♦

4

Foreign Influences

BACKGROUND

Almost inevitably foreign powers will be tempted to intervene in a state torn by internal minority problems. Over the years the rivals and enemies of Iraq have done just this regarding the Kurdish problem as a way to exert pressure on Baghdad. During the 1950s and 1960s, President Gamal Abdul Nasser of Egypt toyed with supporting the Kurds on a number of occasions as a means to pressure Iraq in pursuit of his pan-Arab designs.[1] Nasser even met with Barzani's sometime representative, Jalal Talabani, in 1963, and announced that he saw nothing excessive in the Kurds' demands. Nasser always had to be cautious, however, lest he be seen as supporting a non-Arab separatist movement against a fellow Arab country, and in the end his flirtation with the Kurds came to nothing.

Iran and Turkey presented more serious issues because they shared common borders with Iraq and also contained large Kurdish minorities of their own. Since a Kurdish revolt in any of these three states could well foment one in the others, the three usually tried to cooperate on the issue. Thus the Saadabad Pact in 1937 and the Baghdad Pact in 1955 in part obligated the three to cooperate on the Kurdish issue.[2] This collaboration included measures to prevent cross-border communication and support among the Kurds and, in general, sought to prevent any joint, transnational Kurdish action that might challenge their current international boundaries.

These understandings were disturbed when the Iraqi monarchy was overthrown in 1958. In time, Iran grew alarmed at the rise of Arab nationalism in Iraq and the possibility that these nationalistic feelings might be directed at its Arab-populated province of Khuzistan and the Gulf. In addition, given Iraq's weakness during the 1960s, Iran began to seek to amend the 1937 treaty that gave Iraq the entire Shatt al-Arab River, which served as their common border in the south. Increasingly, therefore, the Shah of Iran began to see the Kurdish card as a way to pressure Iraq. With this background, the United States, an ally of Iran, entered the picture.

THE UNITED STATES

After General Abdul Karim Kassem came to power in 1958, he soon gained the animus of the United States by restoring diplomatic relations with the Soviet Union, lifting the ban on the ICP, and suppressing pro-Western parties. This occurred during the period in which the CIA attempted to assassinate a number of troublesome world leaders, including Patrice Lumumba, Rafael Trujillo, Fidel Castro, and Ngo Dinh Diem.

In February 1960, the chief of the CIA's Directorate for Plans, Near East Division, proposed that Kassem be assassinated with a poisoned handkerchief prepared by that organization's Technical Services Division.[3] Two months later Richard Helms, the chief of operations of the Directorate for Plans and the future director of the CIA, endorsed this proposal as "highly desirable." Although the handkerchief was sent to Kassem, it is not known whether it actually reached him. Certainly it did not kill him; the job was accomplished by his own countrymen three years later. The CIA role in Iraq was to take a different turn.

As early as 1962, Mulla Mustafa Barzani reportedly told New York Times correspondent Dana Adams Schmidt: "Let the Americans give us military aid, openly or secretly, so that we can become truly autonomous, and we will become your loyal partners in the Middle East."[4] In time, the United States and Iran were to exercise an important and eventually tragic foreign influence on the Iraqi Kurds.

The details of the American role were revealed by the Village Voice's unauthorized publication of the Pike House Committee Report investigating the CIA.[5] This document shows that in May 1972, the Shah of Iran, who already was supporting Barzani because Iran and Iraq "had long been bitter enemies," asked U.S. President Richard M. Nixon and soon-to-be Secretary of State Henry Kissinger—who were returning from a Moscow summit meeting—to help him in this project.

Although the U.S. aid was "largely symbolic,"[6] "the United States acted, in effect, as a guarantor that the insurgent group [the Kurds] would not be summarily dropped by the foreign head of state [the Shah]." The Pike Committee Report explained that "on numerous occasions the leader of the ethnic group [Barzani] expressed his distrust of our allies' [i.e., Iran's] intentions. He did, however, trust the United States as indicated by his frequent statements that 'he trusted no other major power.'" John B. Connally, the former governor of Texas, "personally advised the head of state that the United States would cooperate." Although similar proposals had been turned down three times earlier,[7] Nixon and Kissinger had decided to act now for a variety of reasons, including the following.

The Pike Committee Report concluded that "the project was initiated primarily as a favor to our ally [Iran], who had cooperated with United States intelligence agencies, and who had come to feel menaced by his neighbor [Iraq]." Former U.S. Ambassador William Eagleton, Jr., concurred with these findings when he wrote: "My impression . . . is that by far the most important reason for the US intervention was a desire to respond positively to the Shah's request, which was apparently based on Barzani's insistence that some kind of big power support was needed to balance Iraq's Soviet connection."[8]

Another reason for the U.S. action, which Eagleton alluded to, was the Cold War. A continuing Kurdish insurgency would sap the strength of Iraq, a Soviet ally. Did Nixon and Kissinger—who, as mentioned, were just returning from a summit conference in Moscow—believe they were somehow serving the interests of détente by checkmating the Soviets here?

A third reason for the U.S. support of the Kurds was that a continuing Kurdish problem in Iraq would tie Baghdad's troops down at home and make it less likely that Iraq would enter any future Arab-Israeli conflict. As Kissinger later noted in his memoirs: "The benefit of Nixon's Kurdish decision was apparent in just over a year: Only one Iraqi division was available to participate in the October 1973 Middle East War."[9]

Given this reasoning, the Pike Committee Report argued, "it is particularly ironic that . . . the United States . . . restrained the insurgents [the Kurds] from an all-out offensive on one occasion when such an attack might have been successful because other events were occupying the neighboring country." The reference was to Kissinger's shuttle diplomacy at the end of the October 1973 war and how a Kurdish offensive at that time would have hindered it. Thus, as the report shows, Kissinger had the following message sent to the Kurds: "We do not repeat not consider it advisable for you to undertake the offensive military action that [another government (Israel)] has suggested to you." In his memoirs, however, Kissinger argues "that the decision to discourage the Kurds from launching a diversionary offensive during the October 1973 was based on the unanimous view of our intelligence officials and the Shah that the Kurds would be defeated in such an offensive; this judgment was concurred in by the Israeli government."[10]

Still another reason for the U.S. support of the Kurds concerned the Iraq Petroleum Company, which had just been nationalized. One of Barzani's unfortunate promises was that if he would win his struggle against Baghdad he was "ready to become the 51st state."[11] The Kurdish leader also declared that he would "turn over the oil fields to the United States" and that "the United States could look to a friend in OPEC once oil-rich Kurdistan achieved independence."[12] Thus, by supporting the Kurds, the United States might have helped solve the oil and energy problem it was facing at the time.

To implement this U.S. policy, the normal watchdog procedures for an intelligence operation were suspended: "There was no Forty Committee meeting at which a formal proposal paper containing both pros and cons could be discussed and voted on."[13] The Pike Committee Report declared that "the highly unusual security precautions and the circumvention of the Forty Committee were the product of fears by the President and Dr. Kissinger that details of the project would otherwise leak—a result which by all accounts would have mightily displeased our ally [the Shah]." The secrecy also "was motivated by a desire that the Department of State, which had consistently opposed such ventures in the region, be kept in the dark. . . . Elaborate measures were taken to insure that the Department of State did not gain knowledge of the project." The precautions went so far "that not even the Ambassador to the country involved was to be told. In addition, evidence in the committee files is conflicting on whether Secretary of State William P. Rogers was ever informed."

The problem with all this secrecy was that it prevented more people from being involved in the decision-making process, which might have led to a more rational and honest policy. The Shah's support for the Kurds was an open secret; it is difficult to understand why such elaborate secrecy was thought necessary to disguise it.

The real tragedy of this foreign interference, however, was that it reinforced the Baathist concern that Barzani's ultimate objective was the dismantling of Iraq and thus helped lead to the breakdown of the March Manifesto of 1970. Even more, the U.S.-Iranian aid was never intended to be enough for the Kurds to triumph because, if Barzani were actually to win, the Kurds would no longer be able to play the enervating role against the Baathists the United States and Iran desired. Thus, the United States and Iran actually "hoped that our clients [the Kurds] would not prevail. They preferred instead that the insurgents simply continue a level of hostilities sufficient to sap the resources of our ally's [Iran's] neighboring country [Iraq]."[14] Of course, "this policy was not imparted to our clients, who were encouraged to continue fighting. Even in the context of covert action, ours was a cynical enterprise."

As shrewd and tough as Barzani was in his own mountainous homeland, he was naive and weak when it came to trusting the United States. Indeed, "his admiration for Dr. Kissinger was expressed on two occasions when he sent a gift of three rugs and later on the occasion of Dr. Kissinger's marriage, a gold and pearl necklace."

On March 6, 1975, however, as pointed out earlier, Iran and Iraq signed the Algiers Accord under which Iraq recognized the middle of the Shatt al-Arab River as the boundary between their two states, while Iran undertook to halt its aid to Barzani. "The cut-off of aid . . . came as a severe shock to its [the Kurds'] leadership"[15] and made it impossible for the Kurdish rebellion to continue.

Barzani sent the following message to the CIA: "There is confusion and dismay among our people and forces. Our people's fate [is] in unprecedented danger. Complete destruction [is] hanging over our head. . . . We appeal [to] you . . . [to] intervene according to your promises." The Kurdish leader also appealed to Kissinger: "We feel your Excellency that the United States has a moral and political responsibility towards our people who have committed themselves to your country's policy."

Despite these pleas, "the U.S. [even] refused to extend humanitarian assistance to the thousands of refugees created by the abrupt termination of military aid." As the Pike Committee Report explained, the United States had become such "junior partners" of the Shah, that it "had no choice but to acquiesce" to his cutting off Barzani's support.

At the time, Barzani justified his disastrous reliance on the Shah and the United States by arguing that "a drowning man stretches his hand out for everything"[16]; later, however, in exile, he admitted: "Without American promises, we would never have become trapped and involved to such an extent."[17] In reply, Kissinger simply stated that "covert action should not be confused with missionary work."[18] In April 1991 the Iraqi Kurds were to learn this lesson again.

Other Reasons

At first glance, it seems difficult to understand how Barzani had become so hopelessly dependent on Iranian aid that he could not continue without it, when all through the 1960s he had managed to battle Baghdad to a standstill on his own. The explanation is multifaceted.

First of all, of course, Barzani had received some earlier aid from the Iranians during the 1960s. This aid had played a secondary role in helping him withstand the government at that time. Much more important, Baghdad governments during the 1960s had been weak and unstable. Thus Barzani had been able to hold out against the central authorities despite their repeated attempts to subdue him. All this began to change dramatically in July 1968, when the Baathists returned to power and constructed a much more stable and modern political and military infrastructure than had previously existed. By 1975 the institutional prerequisites for subduing the Kurds were in place and Barzani's career came to a quick end.

The reliance on Iranian and United States aid led to such self-assurance that nothing was done to win over progressive Arab, European, or Third-World support. In addition, Barzani called for Kurds throughout Iraq to move to the area he held in the north, where he created a bloated, inefficient bureaucracy that made fighting the war more difficult. Overzealous denunciations of the government's bombing attacks created panics that triggered mass refugee problems. Finally, the heavy weapons received from Iran lulled Barzani into trying to maintain fixed lines and fighting a conventional war that he could not win given the government's newfound energy.[19]

ISRAEL

Israel, perceiving itself in a precarious position amid the Arab world and particularly threatened by Iraq's frequent hostility toward its very existence, inevitably took an interest in the Kurdish problem as a possible way to divert Iraqi resources and antagonism from itself. Even before the creation of the State of Israel, the Jewish Agency planted an operative in Baghdad.[20] From there, under journalistic cover, Reuven Shiloah, who later became the founder of the Israeli intelligence community, trekked through the mountains of Kurdistan and worked with the Kurds in pursuit of a "peripheral concept" as early as 1931.

During the 1960s, Israeli military advisers trained Kurdish guerrillas as a way to reduce the potential military threat Iraq presented to the Jewish state and also to help Iraqi Jews escape to Israel. This training operation was code-named "Marvad" (Carpet). In the mid-1960s Shimon Peres, the Israeli deputy minister of defense and later prime minister, met secretly with Kumran Ali Bedir-Khan, a Kurdish leader who had spied for the Israelis in the 1940s and 1950s. Aryeh (Lova) Eliav, an Israeli Cabinet member, personally rode a mule over the mountains in 1966 to deliver a field hospital to the Kurds. The important defection of an Iraqi air force MiG pilot and his plane to Israel in August 1966 was effected with Kurdish help, while Israeli officers apparently assisted Barzani in his major victory over Baghdad at Mt. Hindarin in May 1966.

Following the Six Days War in 1967, Israeli assistance for the Kurds increased considerably. Yaakov Nimrodi, the influential Israeli military attaché in Tehran, served as the main channel. At times, Israeli advisers wore Iranian uniforms. In September 1967 Barzani visited Israel and presented Moshe Dayan, the Israeli defense minister, with a curved Kurdish dagger. Barzani found Israeli mortars superior to those he had been using and asked for more. Many believed that a particularly successful Kurdish mortar attack on the oil refineries at Kirkuk in March 1969 was the work of the Israelis. Israeli officers helping the Kurds remained in constant radio contact with Israel.

Basing his story on a CIA account, American reporter Jack Anderson wrote: "Every month . . . a secret Israeli envoy slips into the mountains in northern Iraq to deliver $50,000 to Mulla Mustafa al-Barzani. . . . The subsidy ensures Kurdish hostility against Iraq, whose government is militantly anti-Israel."[21] Former Israeli Prime Minister Menachem Begin admitted that his country gave the Kurds "money, arms, and instructors."[22]

Writing about the 1960s, Sa'ad Jawad, an authority on the Iraqi Kurds, concluded that "it is an open secret that they [the Israelis] sent some sophisticated weapons through Iran, particularly anti-tank and anti-aircraft equipment, accompanied by instructors." He added that "some Kurds had military training in Israel, while several KDP leaders made visits to Israel and high-ranking Israeli officials to Kurdistan."[23] Both the Israeli Mossad and the Iranian Savak helped Barzani establish "a sophisticated intelligence apparatus, Parastin [Security] . . . to gather information on the Iraqi government and its armed forces."[24] As recently as 1990, it was understood that the Mossad still maintained contacts with the Iraqi Kurds.[25]

♦ ♦ ♦

5

After the Fall

After Barzani's collapse in 1975, his KDP broke into several factions.[1] One joined a KDP splinter already cooperating with Baghdad. Prominent members of this group included: (1) Habib Muhammad Karim, the former secretary-general of the KDP who had been nominated by it to be the vice president of Iraq under the terms of the March Manifesto of 1970 but had been rejected because of his Iranian heritage; (2) Aziz Aqrawi, the general secretary of this KDP splinter who later fled from Baghdad in 1980 and joined the Socialist Party of Kurdistan; (3) Dara Tawfiq, a former member of the ICP and later member of the KDP Politburo who also had been editor of the KDP newspaper Al-Taakhi and had been sent to Baghdad in 1969 to negotiate with Saddam; and (4) Hasim Aqrawi (no relationship to Aziz) who was the president of the Executive Council of the "Autonomous Region" set up by Baghdad in 1974.

Dr. Mahmud Uthman, a physician from Sulaymaniya who had been a top Barzani aide as a member of the KDP Politburo from 1964 on and had played a key role in negotiating the March Manifesto of 1970, also broke with Barzani. Uthman escaped to Europe where he wrote a stinging critique against his erstwhile leader. Later he established his own party, the KDP/Preparatory Committee. At first based in Damascus, Uthman moved back into northern Iraq in 1978. The following year he joined Rasul Mamand to form the United Socialist Party of Kurdistan.[2] In 1981 the party adopted its present name, the Socialist Party of Kurdistan in Iraq (SPKI).

The real heirs of Barzani's KDP proved to be his two loyal sons, the half brothers Massoud and Idris. In Iran they joined another former associate of their father, Muhammad Mahmud Abd al- Rahman, popularly known as "Sami," to form the KDP/Provisional Command (KDPPC) in November 1975. The members of this KDP offshoot were mainly from the far northern regions of Northern Kurmanji-speaking Iraq and felt a strong personal loyalty to the Barzani family. Although both Barzanis relied on traditional tribal ties as their base of support, Massoud tended to be the military commander, while Idris acted as the political negotiator in Tehran and also handled foreign affairs.

At its ninth congress held in Iran in 1979, internal conflicts between the progressive Sami and the traditionalist Idris, who supported Islamic Iran, led to Sami leaving the party to establish his own Kurdistan Popular Democratic Party (KPDP), or People's Party of Kurdistan. At the same time, the young Barzanis reassumed the old KDP name. Although it has never regained the overall position it had under Mulla Mustafa Barzani in the early 1970s, in time this new KDP grew to become the strongest Kurdish party in Iraq. After Idris died of an apparent heart attack in 1987, Massoud became its sole leader.

Jalal Talabani's Patriotic Union of Kurdistan (PUK) represented yet another faction from the old KDP. As described in Chapter 3, this party was really the heir of the old KDP Politburo, which had battled against Mulla Mustafa in the earlier years. Along with the new KDP, Talabani's PUK was to become the other major Kurdish party in Iraq.

Shortly after the Baathist victory in March 1975, Talabani canvassed Kurds who had been able to escape from Iraq. In June 1976 he announced the creation of the PUK in Damascus. Although the PUK adopted the same slogan as the KDP—"autonomy for Kurdistan, democracy for Iraq" —it advocated Marxist principles and denounced the Barzanis as "reactionary." In 1976 the PUK also became the first Kurdish party to return peshmergas to Iraq. The KDP followed and soon the two groups had several hundred, highly mobile guerrillas who were able to mount raids far from their bases.

For its part, Baghdad did not sit idly by. As one observer noted: "In the immediate aftermath of the collapse, it followed a soft-line policy in order to absorb and utilise the Kurdish masses' disillusionment and bitterness against their leadership."[3] The Baathists instituted a modest autonomy in a portion of the traditional Kurdish homeland. A number of economic development projects also were begun that benefited many segments of the population.

The Autonomous Region of Kurdistan established in 1974 constituted only approximately half the territory Barzani had claimed.[4] The institutional structure was located in Arbil and included an Executive Council of as many as twelve members who exercised both executive and legislative power, and a Legislative Assembly of eighty who acted in an advisory capacity to the council. Although the Autonomy Law provided for the election of the assembly, Baghdad actually appointed most of its members from the large landowners and traditional tribal chiefs who could be counted on to be subservient. What is more, the powers of this "autonomous government" were so severely limited that most Kurds saw it as merely a puppet of Baghdad. Indeed, by 1977 it no longer even was referred to as the "Autonomous Region of Kurdistan," but simply as the "Autonomous Region."

While Baghdad offered the Kurds the carrot of "autonomy," it also set about implementing the stick of "Arabization" by moving Arabs into traditional Kurdish lands, while at the same time creating a "Kurd-free" buffer zone along the northeastern corner of the country. Kurdish sources claim that in the process more than 3,000 villages eventually were destroyed and 500,000 people forcibly moved to the plains of southern Kurdistan or to the south of Iraq.[5] Among other things, this buffer zone would cut the Iraqi Kurds off from their kinsmen in Turkey, Iran, and Syria as well as insulate Iraq from cross-border attacks.

The government argued, however, that its purpose was to relocate the Kurds into newer housing where they would have better access to water, electricity, and schools. Illustrative of what Baghdad probably really intended, however, one Kurdish spokesman replied that:

> The Kurds have a saying: "Level the mounts, and in a day the Kurds would be no more." To a Kurd the mountain is no less than the embodiment of the deity: mountain is his mother, his refuge, his protector, his home, his farm, his market, his mate—and his only friend. . . . Kurds who settle in the cities outside the mountains—even those within Kurdistan proper—soon lose their true Kurdish identities.[6]

Still another Kurdish observer explained:

> The villages of Kurdistan have evolved out of a centuries-old equilibrium between man and nature. Each mountain village has its stream or river, its field, its orchards, its cemetery and, often enough, its oak forest. The strategic hamlets are like an oven in the summer and freezing cold in the winter. They represent an inadmissibly brutal intrusion into the life of a society whose equilibrium they will disrupt.[7]

Clearly, resentment at the forced deportations fed the resumption of guerrilla warfare.

In the fall of 1977 the PUK moved its headquarters from Damascus to the Sorani-speaking areas of the Sulaymaniya region south of the KDP strongholds. Arms and supplies, however, had to come from Syria through Turkey by way of KDP-controlled areas. Early in 1978, therefore, Talabani sent many of his best fighters to facilitate this movement. The KDP felt threatened and dealt a bitter defeat to the PUK, whose men did not know the terrain. Ali al-Askari, who had been widely respected as one of Mulla Mustafa Barzani's most capable commanders and had become a prominent leader of the PUK after 1975, was one of those killed in this intra-Kurdish bloodletting. It took the PUK several years to recover from the blow, but the Kurdish movement long remained divided between these two poles. Indeed even in 1993, the unity that has been achieved remains fragile.

Early in 1979, Ayatollah Ruhollah Khomeini overthrew the Shah and established a fundamentalist, Islamic government in Iran. This regime either did not want to or could not enforce the provisions of the Algiers Agreement on preventing cross-border Kurdish activities. The Iraqi Kurds and especially the KDP established bases in Iran again to challenge Baghdad, a situation that helped lead to the Iran-Iraq War.

♦ ♦ ♦

6

The Iran–Iraq Gulf War

In September 1980 Iraq invaded Iran.[1] After initial Iraqi successes, the war bogged down into a long stalemate and thus created tremendous potential opportunities for the Kurdish national movement in Iraq. Indeed, for much of the 1980s, the Iraqi Kurds partially ruled themselves as Saddam fought for his very existence against the attacking Iranians. On the other hand, however, both Iran and Iraq began to use each other's Kurds as a fifth column. Eventually, continuing Kurdish divisions and the end of the war dealt another cruel blow to the Kurdish hopes.[2]

In Iraq, the KDP supported Iran and at times acted almost as advance units for its invading armies. The PUK, on the other hand, wavered between the two antagonists, breaking off negotiations with Baghdad only at the end of 1984. For their part, the Iranian Kurds—tragically but understandably—supported Iraq. Thus, the war saw Iraqi Kurds fighting not only against each other but also Iranian Kurds.

Until 1983, northern Iraq was largely quiet. The Iranian attacks in the south forced Baghdad to deploy most of its troops there and thus grant some de facto control to the Kurds in the north. Indeed many Kurds who earlier had been deported to the south were permitted to return to their northern homes. Housed at first in camps, thousands began to escape to areas controlled by the KDP and PUK.

In November 1980 the PUK joined with the Socialist Party of Kurdistan in Iraq (SPKI), led by Rasul Mamand and Mahmud Uthman, and the Iraqi Communist Party (ICP), led since 1964 by Aziz Muhammad who himself was a Kurd, as well as several other smaller groups, to form the Democratic National and Patriotic Front (DNPF). The KDP was purposely omitted. It responded by excluding the PUK when it joined with the two main partners of the PUK in the so-called Democratic National Front (DNF) a few weeks later. The result was a continuance of the traditional Kurdish inability to unite. Indeed, following armed clashes in 1983 between the PUK and the SPKI, their front disintegrated, and the SPKI moved closed to the KDP.

Still another front was created in July 1981 by a dissident, former Baathist, general, Hassan Mustafa al-Naqib. This organization was known as either the Islamic National Liberation Front or the Iraqi Front of Revolutionary, Islamic, and National Forces. Although a great deal of publicity was given to these three fronts, in reality they accomplished little at the time. Arguably, however, they did set the precedent for the unity that was finally achieved in the late 1980s with the creation of the Iraqi Kurdistan Front.

During the first few years of the war, relations between the KDP and the PUK alternated greatly. At first they managed to get along rather well, because both, after all, had the same goal of overthrowing the Baathist government and establishing an autonomous Kurdistan within a democratic Iraq. By the fall of 1981, however, their relationship had degenerated into open conflict, largely because of the KDP's support of Iran. Following an ICP appeal for unity, this conflict ceased by the summer of 1982. In August the KDP and the PUK were able to carry out a joint operation in the Sulaymaniya area.

Iran's major Haj Omran offensive into northern Iraq, which began on July 21, 1983, however, led to new misunderstandings and hostilities between the two. The KDP saw the situation as an opportunity to magnify its armed opposition to Baghdad with Iranian aid in concert with such other dissident Iraqi groups as the Shiite Dawa Party (Party of the Islamic Call), which had been founded in the holy city of Najaf in 1964. The PUK, however, believed that in such a moment of weakness, Iraq would be more willing to negotiate a favorable deal. Indeed, the defeats on the front and unrest among the Kurds had already caused Saddam to begin to try to appease them.

Baghdad reemphasized the rights already enjoyed by its Kurds and the threat fundamentalist Iran represented. This point concerning Iran appealed particularly to the PUK's more secular emphasis rather than the more traditionalist KDP. Kurds accused of antigovernment activities (but who were not responsible for killings) were pardoned. Kurdish soldiers who had deserted from the Iraqi army were granted amnesty, and the government even ruled that they could serve in what until the summer of 1983 had been the relatively quiet north. In August 1983 elections took place for the Legislative Council of the Kurdish autonomous region. Although the results were still rigged, the resulting council was more favorable to the Kurdish nationalists than the previous council appointed by the Baathists.

As the combined Iranian-KDP offensive forced the PUK out of its sanctuary and deeper into Iraq, the PUK and the Iraqi government agreed to a cease-fire in December 1983. With the help of Baghdad's Iranian Kurdish ally, Abdul Rahman Ghassemlou, the leader of the Kurdish Democratic Party of Iran (KDPI), Baghdad and the PUK then signed a "Comprehensive Political and Security Agreement."

At first Iraq seemingly agreed to alter the autonomy law in favor of the Kurds and to extend it to other areas. Although the PUK came under heavy criticism from its former allies in the DNPF, as well as the KDP, for dealing with Baghdad, it replied that the cease-fire offered it a necessary breathing space and the chance to achieve longstanding Kurdish goals.

It is doubtful, however, that either Baghdad or the PUK viewed their negotiations as anything more than a way to gain time. Although they continued to talk until October 1984, the PUK finally terminated the dialogue at the beginning of the following year. The failure was due to a number of different causes. One reason was Turkish-Iraqi cooperation and joint action against both the Turkish and Iraqi Kurds. Iraq also began to receive help from the United States, France, and the Soviet Union to avoid defeat by Iran. Thus, Saddam's hand was strengthened. Another reason was Baghdad's refusal to abandon its irregular Kurdish allies, derisively termed the josh (donkeys) by the Kurdish nationalists, but known as the "Light Brigades" and "Saladin Knights" by the government. Still a further factor was the execution of twenty-four young Kurds in March 1984, for desertion and draft avoidance, as well as the shooting of several Kurdish students at Arbil University. In addition, government forces also shot Talabani's brother, Shaikh Hama Salih, and his two daughters.

The Iraqi Kurdistan Front

Following the failure of the Iraqi-PUK negotiations, the PUK began to bury the hatchet with the KDP. By 1986 a KDP official declared: "We are not enemies anymore, but we cannot be considered loyal friends either. So far as we know [Talabani] fights against the Iraqi government."[3]

This understanding was broadened into the Iraqi Kurdistan Front (Kurdish Front) that was announced in principle in July 1987 and formally in May 1988, with the addition, over the years, of six other, smaller groups: (1) the Socialist Party of Kurdistan in Iraq (SPKI) led by Rasul

Mamand, with Mahmud Uthman as a prominent member; (2) the
Kurdistan Popular Democratic Party (KPDP) or People's Party of
Kurdistan led by Muhammad Mahmud "Sami" Abd al-Rahman; (3) the
Kurdish Socialist Party (PASOK) headed, in effect, by a collective lead-
ership; (4) the Kurdistan Branch or Section of the Iraqi Communist
Party (ICP) led by Aziz Muhammad; (5) the Assyrian Democratic
Movement; and (6) the Kurdistan Toilers Party led by Kadir Jabari.

On the other hand, the Kurdish Islamic Movement led by Shaikh
Uthman Abdul Aziz and the Kurdistan Islamic Party (PIK) have been
specifically mentioned as not belonging to the Front. Similarly, a group
called the Hizbullahs of Kurdistan and led by Shaikh Muhammad
Khalid Barzani, the son of Shaikh Ahmad Barzani and thus the cousin
of Massoud Barzani, is also not a member. In addition, although it has
cooperated with the Front, the National Turkoman[4] Party of Iraq (IMTP)
led by Muzaffer Aslan, is also not a member.

Upon its creation, the Front declared that its main goals were to overthrow the Baathist regime of Saddam Hussein, establish a genuinely
democratic government in Iraq, and develop a federal status for the
Kurds in Iraq.[5] Talabani and Barzani became its co-presidents, with the
former responsible for foreign relations and the latter domestic matters.
Thus, the PUK leader continued to live in Damascus, while travelling to
the United States, Britain, France, West Germany, Iran, and Spain,
among numerous other nations. Although he too occasionally ventured
abroad, Barzani spent most of his time in the mountainous area of
northeastern Iraq.

Renewed Fighting

Even though Baghdad diverted more troops and resources to the Kurdish region, by the autumn of 1985 the KDP had up to 12,000 peshmergas along the Turkish border, where it held a large section of territory
from Syria in the west to Rawanduz in the east. The KDP also gained
strength from its alliance with the Partiya Karkaren Kurdistan (PKK), or
Kurdish Workers Party in Turkey. In May 1985 the KDP claimed to have
achieved a major victory over the government's troops around the mountain village of Mangish not far from the Turkish border. This success was
accomplished with the aid of Iranian irregulars or Pasdaran, creating a
pattern that was followed frequently in the latter years of the war.

As many as 10,000 PUK to the south controlled the roads and rural
areas between Kirkuk and Sulaymaniya as well as the territory up to the
Iranian border at Hawraman. Better weapons were also reaching the

Iraqi Kurds from Libya and Syria through their Iranian ally. One report stated that "Kurdish guerrillas are reported to have been equipped with hand-held Soviet anti-aircraft missiles and even small artillery pieces."[6] Fuad Masum, a senior member of the PUK Politburo, added that "we are indebted to the Iraqi army. The overwhelming proportion of our small arms is captured from Iraq, together with over 700 vehicles. And what we don't take, they sell us."[7]

In February 1986 the Iraqis and their anti-Iranian Kurdish allies were forced from several villages in the area of Sulaymaniya. New offensives in January and March 1987 carried the Iranians to within sixty miles of Kirkuk. In September KDP forces struck at Kanimasi near the Turkish border, capturing equipment and briefly occupying the town.[8] During the winter of 1987-88, the PUK fought alongside Iranian troops in the mountains northeast of Kirkuk. Iran claimed the seizure of some 100 square miles in that area, including twenty-nine strategic heights and six villages on both sides of the Little Zab River. One observer concluded that "by day the Iraqi army patrols the roads; at night, towns, roads and the countryside are in the hands of the peshmerga."[9]

Early in 1988 the KDP claimed to have captured the northern border town of Deirlouk, demolishing an Iraqi intelligence center, the local Baathist headquarters, and the district governor's office. At the end of January the PUK claimed "one of their greatest victories"[10] when it captured a summer palace of Saddam as well as Sari Rash, an Iraqi summer capital. It was reported that Saddam's palace had been burned down during the fierce two-day battle and that thousands of weapons, including antiaircraft guns, heavy machine guns, thirty-six officers, and numerous troops also had been captured.

Talabani claimed that this success was revenge for the Iraqi capture of Mulla Mustafa Barzani's headquarters in 1975. He then went on to speculate about the chances of Kurdish independence.[11] "Whatever happens in the Gulf War . . . we are going to have our own republic. . . . But whether it will be an independent state or a federal part of the state of Iraq will depend on what happens in Baghdad." The PUK leader then elaborated: "If President Saddam Hussein and his Ba'ath Party survive, we will have no alternative but to break away."

By 1988 one observer wrote that "the united strength of the resistance forces amounts to 60,000 armed guerrilla soldiers (20,000 regular and 40,000 people's armed militia of armed peasants)."[12] Another wrote that "by early 1988, Kurdish guerrillas in Iraq were in control of a region covering 3,800 sq. miles."[13]

TURKEY'S ROLE

Over the years other states with Kurdish populations have opposed Kurdish yearnings for independence in Iraq, viewing them as having the potential to set a dangerous precedent. Turkey, in particular, has always seen any manifestation of Kurdish nationalism within its borders as a mortal danger to its territorial integrity. As noted in Chapter 5, Turkey, Iraq, and Iran all agreed to cooperate on the Kurdish question in the Saadabad Pact of 1937 and the Baghdad Pact of 1955.

During the Iran-Iraq War, the PKK began a Kurdish insurgency in Turkey.[14] By 1986 the Kurdish Workers Party (PKK) had concluded an alliance with the KDP that allowed the Kurdish insurgents in Turkey to maintain positions across the border in the KDP-controlled areas of northern Iraq. On a least four separate occasions during the 1980s (May 1983, October 1984, August 1986, and March 1987), Turkish forces crossed the border in pursuit of Kurdish guerrillas. These actions were taken under the terms of an agreement reached in 1981 and in 1984 with Iraq, stating that either could pursue Kurdish guerrillas across their common border.[15] Under entirely different circumstances—given the results of the 1991 Gulf War—Turkish troops once again pursued PKK guerrillas into northern Iraq in August and October 1991 and October 1992.

During the 1986 raid, at least 150 Kurds were killed.[16] Turkish Prime Minister Turgut Ozal announced that three camps housing 100 guerrillas had been destroyed and declared: "We are determined to follow these rebels to their lairs and smash them."[17] Implicitly affirming charges that fighters from the KDP were also among the casualties, Ozal added: "Let this [be] a warning to those who shelter the rebels." Although the KDP threatened to respond, Ankara's firmness apparently was an important factor influencing the KDP eventually to reassess its alliance with the PKK.

Turkey was also drawn to northern Iraq by the unwanted possibility of an Iranian victory. Such an occurrence might have left Khomeini's brand of Islamic fundamentalism and/or some type of an independent Kurdish state in control of the oil-rich area that Turkey still viewed as having been taken away from it in a moment of weakness after World War I.[18] For these reasons, Turkish military intervention seemed possible.

Of immediate concern, however, was the strategic pipeline that carried a million barrels of oil a day from Kirkuk to Iskenderun (Yumurtalik) in Turkey. This pipeline met one-third of Turkey's oil needs and also provided some $300 million in Iraqi rental fees. After Khomeini's government threatened to strike the pipeline in its attempt to launch an offensive into northern Iraq, Turkish authorities warned Iran. A Turkish official described as "unfortunate" Iran's refusal to guarantee the integrity of the pipeline because his country could not remain a spectator if its "crucial interests" were harmed.

In August 1987 Turkish border officials in Hakkari province intercepted a special operations company of the Iranian Revolutionary Guards Corps near Semdinli and took into custody ninety-five prisoners. Turkish officials claimed that the Iranians were trying to sabotage the pipeline, but the Iranians protested they were merely trying to attack a hostile Kurdish guerrilla camp in northern Iraq. The Turks repatriated the prisoners after diplomatic discussions.

The Turkish press speculated about a possible Turkish military operation to save the pipeline from Iranian forces and their Iraqi Kurdish allies, Barzani's KDP, which supported the PKK until the end of 1987. Turkish military sources stated privately they were studying possible options, including the military one.

Huseyin Avni Guler, a former Turkish intelligence officer, and Hassan Isik, a former Turkish foreign minister, claimed to have evidence that the United States was encouraging Turkey to undertake military action if Iran attacked Kirkuk and the pipeline. Such a move would have prevented Iran and possibly Syria from occupying the area and thus depriving Turkey, a NATO ally of the United States, of its use.

Most observers, however, felt that such Turkish action was highly unlikely given the country's vulnerable frontier with the Soviet Union, serious problems with Greece, and continuing occupation of northern Cyprus, not to mention the certain opposition of both Syria and Iran. Nevertheless, if the Iran-Iraq Gulf War suddenly had taken a disastrous turn for Iraq, as many for long predicted, the Mosul-Kirkuk area would have become a rich, strategic, political, and economic vacuum that might well have drawn the Turks in. Of course, Iraq did not collapse, and, with the end of the war in the summer of 1988 and the reassertion of Iraqi authority in its Kurdish north, the entire question became moot.

HALABJA

To help stem the Iranian onslaught, Baghdad began to resort to chemical warfare as early as 1983.[19] One observer asserted that "from April 1987, the Iraqi government has started to extensively bombard different areas of Iraqi Kurdistan with chemical weapons (mustard, nerve, and cyanide) every time it suffers a big military defeat at the hands of the

Kurdish partisans."[20] Such attacks had occurred at Sheikh Wesanan, Balisan, Bote, Garmyan, Yakhsamar, Karadagh, and Sargaloo.

Another report argued that "no fewer than 67 incidents of chemical weapon attacks were reported from April 1987 to April 1988, mostly in northern Iraq, and directed against Kurdish civilians quite as much as Pesh Mergas."[21] Jalal Talabani claimed the Iraqis used chemical warfare fired from artillery or dropped from planes against the Kurds on February 26, 27, and 28, 1988, in the Balisan and Jaffati valleys, killing twelve civilians and injuring 210, and added that: "They use chemical weapons all the time, especially when waging big attacks."[22]

On March 16, 1988, as many as 5,000 people were killed in Halabja, an Iraqi Kurdish city of some 70,000 situated approximately 15 miles from the border with Iran and 150 miles northeast of Baghdad, when that city suffered the most notorious gas attack since World War I.[23] Kurdish peshmergas had just captured the town as part of a large offensive by the Iranian army that had penetrated up to thirty miles into Iraq. Iraqi forces in the vicinity had surrendered or withdrawn.

At approximately 2:00 P.M., a single Iraqi warplane appeared from the west and dropped one or more bombs that spread a yellow and white cloud throughout the city. Reports indicated that the gas was a combination of mustard gas and possibly some other, more instantly fatal agent. According to medical personnel in Tehran who treated some survivors, the gas cloud contained a mixture of mustard and cyanide gases. The victims showed the classic symptoms of mustard gas effects, ugly skin lesions and breathing difficulties.

Halabja proved to be part of the beginning of Iraq's 1988 offensive that eventually forced Iran to agree to a cease-fire on August 20. Thus freed, from the war Baghdad turned on its Kurdish rebels and quickly routed them.

The United States State Department claimed that "on several days in August, chemical weapons were used in this campaign."[24] In October a delegation of three United States doctors representing the Physicians for Human Rights examined some of the victims and "concluded that chemical weapons were used by Iraq in attacks on Kurdish villages on August 25, 1988. . . . In particular, history and physical signs are most consistent with either a combination of a vesicant (blistering agent) and a more rapidly acting lethal agent (such as nerve gas), or a single vesicant agent that rapidly causes death."[25]

Akram Mayi, a Kurdish leader who later escaped to the United States, remembered: "On 28 August 1988, they [the Iraqis] started bombing. They dropped chemical weapons on 70 points. . . . The color of the gas was between white and yellow. . . . It smelled of garlic. Thousands of men and women and children died."[26]

REFUGEES

As a result of this Iraqi action, at least 60,000 Kurdish refugees fled across the Turkish border in September 1988. There they faced an uncertain future in squalid tent cities. In addition, Baghdad declared that the refugees were "terrorists and criminals" and that it was "sorry for Ankara's decision"[27] to offer them sanctuary. The Turkish prime minister, Turgut Ozal, responded, however, that: "We will do all we can for the Iraqi Kurds,"[28] while Kamran Inan, the cabinet minister in charge of eastern affairs and himself an ethnic Turkish Kurd, added in criticism of the lack of Western material support: "We are trying to carry this burden alone."[29]

For the Turks, the real problem was what to do with the Kurdish refugees in the long run. Already Turkey was burdened by its own Kurdish (PKK) insurgency, so leaders there feared that some of the incoming Iraqi Kurds might link up with these insurgents. After most of the refugees turned down Iraq's offer of amnesty and the excitement of the first few days began to wear off, more and more Turks began to express reservations about the situation.

By mid-October the refugees were dying from the cold at the rate of eight to ten a day.[30] Most of the dead were children, because they were the ones least adequately dressed and most prone to hypothermia. Already temperatures were falling below freezing at night, and too few blankets were available. The head of one family said: "It is freezing cold at night and there is not room for everyone to sleep in the tents." When nearly 1,000 of the refugees did accept Iraq's offer of amnesty, Barzani loyalists tried to prevent their convoy from leaving by stoning it. In addition, the areas between the tents were virtually open sewers.

By spring 1989 the refugees felt that they were "the near- forgotten."[31] Housed in a tent city and overcrowded apartment blocks, the first week of February alone, 349 died, 269 of them children. The Turks refused to grant the refugees official refugee status because of the attendant costs and political repercussions. Instead they argued that they were doing the best they could with the limited resources available. They blamed the West for lecturing them about the situation, while offering little in tangible help.

Nevertheless, one report concluded, "the Kurds seem to have enough to eat, although . . . there are problems, too, with nonworking heating systems, water taps and toilets. . . . As a group, they seem in good health and are receiving adequate medical care."[32] The Turks were said to have done their best with the limited resources they had.

In the summer of 1989, the KDP accused Turkey of a "very sinister operation" and "clear hypocrisy" in attempting secretly to send thousands of the refugees into Iran without the permission of that state.[33] (During the previous fall, Iran had already rebuked Turkey for sending more than 20,000 refugees across the border.) Abdulmumin Barzani, the cousin of Massoud, was reported to have travelled to Tehran to seek permission for the remaining refugees to enter the country. Turkey denied that any Kurds had been forced into Iran, claiming that those who had entered did so voluntarily.[34]

In the spring of 1991, approximately 30,000 refugees still remained in Turkey, when the failure of that year's uprising brought a new, much larger wave of several hundred thousand more up to the Turkish border.

RELOCATION

Given the KDP's and PUK's role as fifth columns during the Iran-Iraq War, the Baathists decided to renew their efforts to relocate significant numbers of Kurds, a policy initiated in the 1970s or even earlier. The apparent purpose was to preempt future Kurdish uprisings by thinning the population along the borders and moving it to areas where it could be diluted and more easily controlled by the government. In some cases Arab settlers were even moved in to replace the departed Kurds, but the mountainous climate usually did not suit them, and the attempt at Arabization foundered.

According to Vera Beaudin Saeedpour, a leading spokeswoman for the Kurds, an Arabization policy had been attempted as early as 1963, by "forcibly removing Kurdish inhabitants from the oil-rich regions of Kirkuk, Khanakin, Kifri and the plains of Arbil. Shortly thereafter, Kurds east of Mosul city, Ein Zaleh and Sinjar were displaced."[35] Following the defeat of Mulla Mustafa Barzani in 1975, "security belts" some twenty kilometers (thirteen miles) wide were created along Iraq's borders stretching from Mandali in the south to Shangur in the northwest, as discussed in Chapter 5. In these areas the Kurdish population was reportedly totally removed and water sources poisoned or cemented over.

In April 1982 "Sami's" KPDP reported that "one of the long-term strategic policy objectives of the present Iraqi regime is the destruction of the national identity of the Kurdish people in Iraq."[36] One of the main ways to accomplish this "is the displacement of the Kurds living in Kurdistan—by dispersing them in the central and southern provinces of

Iraq—and the mass deportation to Iran of the Kurds living in the other areas of the country."[37]

On the eve of the 1991 War, Jalal Talabani declared that after the Iran-Iraq War "more than 5,000 Kurdish villages were razed by the [Iraqi] Army. Some two million Kurds now live in concentration camps at the edges of the major cities in Kurdistan."[38] On the other hand, the U.S. Department of State reported that "an estimated 250,000 to 300,000 Kurdish villagers were forcibly relocated in 1988; since . . . 1987, an estimated 500,000 people have been uprooted."[39]

During the spring and summer of 1989, the Iraqis undertook the depopulation of Qala Diza, a city of over 100,000 only ten miles from the Iranian border.[40] Raniya, a city of some 50,000 ten miles farther to the west, and the densely populated Kurdish communities east of the Dukan Reservoir and ten miles southwest of Qala Diza were scheduled to be next. The Iraqi government considered the territory to be a strategic area in any future conflict against Iran. In addition, of course, the destruction of the Kurdish villages and towns in these remote areas served to deprive the peshmergas of bases of support and hiding in their guerrilla warfare against Baghdad.

New settlements, termed "concentration camps" by Talabani, were constructed in the valleys and dusty plains away from the border. A new Halabja, twelve miles away from the old one and renamed "Saddamite Halabja," was one. The government argued that these new homes had running water, electricity, and Kurdish-language schools, and would thus improve the Kurdish standard of living and help preserve their culture. The Kurds replied that in most cases they already had such facilities and preferred to live in their old homes. The mass exodus of more than a million Kurds into Iran following the failed uprising of March 1991 threatened virtually to eliminate the civilian Kurdish population in northeastern Iraq.

OTHER MEASURES

The Baathist regime has also employed a variety of other measures, including apparent murder, poisoning, and torture. On July 30, 1983, Iraqi security forces rounded up some 8,000 Barzani Kurds between the ages of twelve and eighty who were being held at camps near Arbil. Saddam accused them of being loyal to the KDP, which had helped the Iranians at the Haj Omran offensive a week earlier. The Kurds were taken to Baghdad and never heard of again. It is likely that they were all murdered.[41]

Early in 1988, Amnesty International reported that "hundreds of . . . political prisoners reportedly [were] executed without charge or trial or after summary and secret military hearings."[42] Their bodies were handed back to their families only after payment of the customary official execution fee of up to 300 Iraqi dinars. The executed included eight minors aged fourteen to seventeen.

Amnesty International also reported that thirteen Kurds were "victims of deliberate summary killings by government forces after house-to-house searches and the bombardment of the Kirkuk village of Kiman on November 11, 1987." More than 100 other Kurds were killed during the operation, reported to have been launched after the victims had returned to the village from which they had been evicted.

Another thirty-two Kurds from the town of Shaqlawa in Arbil province were executed as military reprisals in November after peshmergas had killed eight Iraqi officials including the town's mayor. Thirty-one Kurds suspected of sympathizing with the KDP were executed following summary military trials in the same month. Children between the ages of ten and fourteen were arrested in retaliation for the political activities of their relatives; three supposedly died of torture.

In yet another report, Amnesty International declared that the Iraqi government was poisoning some members of the PUK and SPKI with thallium or rat poison.[43] The poison apparently was put into a yogurt drink by a female agent of the government who was working at the home of a PUK member. In this particular instance, three Kurds died, while seven recovered. One of the survivors, PUK member Mustafa Qader Mahmoud, also had been poisoned in an earlier murder attempt.

♦   ♦   ♦

7

The 1991 Gulf War

After the Iran-Iraq War—with its legacy of chemical warfare and refugees—the Kurds were left exhausted and demoralized. Saddam's invasion of Kuwait in August 1990 and the international alliance it provoked, however, once again created new possibilities for the Kurds, since they were obviously potential allies against the Baghdad regime. Amid much speculation, Jalal Talabani journeyed to Washington, but warned: "We have been deceived many times by foreigners. We are determined not to make the same mistakes again."[1] For its part the United States appeared wary of alienating its important Turkish and new Syrian ally, as well as Iran, by supporting the Kurds.

Asked whether the Kurds would join the allies if war broke out, Talabani replied: "We would not," and even threatened that "if the Turkish Army invades Iraq's Kurdistan, we would stand against it."[2] The Kurdish leader softened his position, however, by noting that "we have fought Saddam since he assumed power and will continue to fight him until he is toppled," adding that "if the Arab forces liberate Kuwait, we would urge the Kurdish troops to join them." He maintained, though, that "our fighting would be Kurdish, independent, and separate . . . not . . . as part of foreign armies invading or fighting Iraq."

Despite the golden opportunity the events presented, Talabani continued to maintain a sober attitude: "We don't want to be like the Palestinians and ask for the impossible. If there were a democratic government in Iraq, we would be happy to be Iraqis."[3] Hussein Guzelaydin, a Kurdish refugee who had settled in Canada, also reflected this apparent caution when he stated: "We want U.S. help against Iraq, but we also need guarantees that 1975 won't happen all over again."[4] For his part, Izzat Ibrahim, the deputy chairman of the Baathist's ruling Revolutionary Command Council (RCC), warned the Kurds: "If you have forgotten Halabja, I would like to remind you that we are ready to repeat the operation."[5]

Once the War began in January 1991, however, Talabani declared that "the Kurds are really happy because they believe that this war will put an end to Saddam Husayn's dictatorship."[6] This belief, the fear that they would be left out of the postwar settlement, and the call from U.S. President George Bush for the Iraqis to overthrow Saddam after he was defeated in late February, help to explain why the Kurds rebelled when their earlier statements implied they would not.

FALSE VICTORY

After the rebellion failed, Talabani claimed that "the leadership of the Kurds has never called for an uprising."[7] Instead, he maintained that following "the appeal of the Americans, spontaneous and unorganized demonstrations erupted everywhere. The Peshmerga fighters were outside the towns, and only later did we decide to support the demonstrators."

Although there is probably some truth to Talabani's assertion, it ignores the fact that the Kurdish leadership also had made preparations. One report, for example, indicated "that 2,500 Kurdish guerrillas who had escaped to Syria have infiltrated back into northeastern Iraq,"[8] while another declared that "several thousand Kurdish peshmerga . . . are poised to take control of the biggest population centres of northern Iraq in the event of Saddam Hussein's government collapsing in the face of the allied offensive.[9]

Most of the major cities in Iraqi Kurdistan fell with astounding alacrity to the rebels in early and mid-March: Arbil, Sulaymaniya, Jalula, Dohuk, Zakho, and Kirkuk, among others. Dr. Kamal al-Karkuki, a member of the Central Committee of the KDP, claimed that most of the members of two Iraqi army corps had joined the rebels,[10] while Talabani added that "in the province of Sulaymaniya alone, 43,000 had deserted, and in . . . Karkuk, 29,000."[11]

Massoud Barzani declared: "I feel that the result of 70 years of struggle . . . is at hand now. It is the greatest honor for me. It is what I wanted all my life."[12] One Kurdish radio broadcast exulted: "Our dear listeners, the crucial battle has been decided . . . in the most splendid victory in the contemporary history of the Kurds,"[13] while Hoshyar Zevari, a spokesman for the KDP, asserted: "This is the nearest we've ever come to achieving our objectives."[14]

In Beirut, both the PUK and KDP belonged to the recently established Free Iraqi Council or Joint Action Committee of seventeen, disparate Iraqi opposition groups chaired by Saad Salih Jabr. By the middle of March this group announced plans to establish a provisional government to replace Saddam. Speaking from the offices of the PUK in Damascus, Talabani reiterated that he wanted Iraq to maintain its territorial integrity[15] and claimed that the rebels had liberated "virtually all" of the Kurdish areas of Iraq. He then predicted that the Kurds and Shiite fighters in the south along with the opposition groups would topple Saddam. If the Iraqi leader resorted to chemical weapons, Talabani threatened, "we will blow up the dams and Baghdad will be submerged in water."

On March 26 Talabani left Syria and crossed into northern Iraq in a triumphal motorcade. He entered Zakho to a tumultuous welcome to tell more than 10,000 cheering Kurds: "This is the first time ever that the whole of Iraqi Kurdistan has been liberated."[16] Before captured, heavy Iraqi arms, antiaircraft guns, and recoilless rifles on display in the main square, Talabani then vowed that "we will continue the struggle until we defeat the regime of oppression in Baghdad and liberate the whole of Iraq." He also announced that he would confer with other opposition leaders, some of whom had just arrived with him from Syria, about the formation of an interim government in the Kurdish region.

TALKS WITH THE TURKS

On March 8, 1991, Turkey broke its longstanding policy against negotiating with any Kurdish groups when Ambassador Tugay Ozceri, undersecretary of the foreign ministry, met in Ankara with Jalal Talabani and Mohsin Dizai, an envoy of Barzani. A second meeting between Ozceri and Dizai occurred on March 22. Talabani declared "that a new page had been turned in relations between Turkey and the Kurds of Iraq."[17]

For the first meeting, the two Kurds arrived together in Istanbul on a flight from Damascus and were immediately flown to Ankara's military airport by personnel of the National Intelligence Organization (MIT). After it was over, Talabani said that for the Iraqi Kurds, "the most significant result . . . was Turkey's lifting its objection to the establishment of direct relations between the Kurdish front in Iraq and the United States."[18] He also repeated that the Kurds did not want to establish an independent state in northern Iraq and that he had calmed Turkey's apprehensions in this regard. Talabani then elaborated on the following points:

> Turkey has for years been putting forth effective and significant obstacles to the struggle we have been waging in northern Iraq. We wanted to explain our

goals and eliminate Turkey's opposition. . . . We were received with understanding. . . . I believe that we were able to convince them that we do not pose
a threat to Turkey. . . . Our goal is to establish a federation of Arabs,
Turkomans, and Kurds.[19]

The talks created a furor in Turkey.[20] To some, Turkish President Turgut
Ozal was simply being realistic in seeking to build reasonable relations
with those who looked likely to establish an autonomous Kurdish region
on his state's border. To others, however, he in effect was lending support to circles threatening Turkish territorial integrity. If the Turkish
president could countenance some sort of federal solution for the Kurds
in Iraq, might he not also be contemplating one for the Kurds in Turkey?
Former president Kenan Evren and the current chief of general staff
Dogan Gures both spoke of the possible dangers of the Ozal overture.[21]
The military commanders added that "we believe that there will be subsequent demands and we think that this is harmful to our national integrity."

DEFEAT

Defeat proved as swift as victory. Indeed, in retrospect, the victory had
been false because the territorial gains made by the Kurds had little
strategic importance and could not be held once Saddam subdued the
Shiites in the south and turned his modern army north. In reporting the
Iraqi recapture of Arbil, which for two weeks had served as Barzani's
headquarters and been considered the capital of "liberated Kurdistan,"
the Kurds admitted that they had been "outclassed by the Iraqi Army's
tanks, heavy artillery, and helicopters."[22]

Barzani charged that by permitting Saddam to use helicopters, the
United States had given him the "green light . . . to continue massacring
Iraqi civilians."[23] Mahmud Uthman, a leader of the Socialist Party of
Kurdistan in Iraq (SPKI), declared: "They are bombing us, and using
napalm, and civilian casualties are heavy."[24] He added that the Kurds
were equipped with "many light weapons taken from the enemy," but
lacked more sophisticated weapons such as antiaircraft missiles. Talabani
declared that "the rebels were left in the lurch at the decisive moment,
when . . . Saddam was permitted to use any kind of planes, helicopter,
heavy artillery, gasoline and napalm-phosphorous bombs."[25] Even when
the Kurds were able to capture heavy weapons such as tanks and armored personnel carriers, it was reported that "they don't know how to
use them."[26]

THE U.S. ROLE

With hindsight, only the United States could have helped the Kurds to avert defeat by: (1) continuing its war against Saddam longer so that more of his army would have been destroyed, thus depriving him of the capacity to crush the Kurds; (2) preventing Saddam from using fixed-winged airplanes and helicopters, which were so effective against the Kurds and were supposedly denied Baghdad by the terms of the cease-fire; and (3) giving actual military support to the Kurds. For a variety of reasons none of these options was taken.

The United States originally had justified its decision to halt the war when it did on the grounds that the goal of ejecting Iraq from Kuwait had been achieved, and virtually all the Iraqi armor appeared to be trapped. There was no United Nations (U.N.) mandate to go any further. In addition, the United States did not want to appear to be slaughtering an already beaten enemy.

A month after the cease-fire, however, the United States admitted that "the number of Iraqi tanks and armored vehicles that survived the war is much greater than American military authorities initially reported," adding that "many of the weapons have been used by the Government of President Saddam Hussein to quell resistance by Iraqi insurgents."[27] These new estimates "raise questions about the wisdom of the Bush Administration's decision to halt the ground war . . . when the White House did."

The allied commander, U.S. General Norman Schwarzkopf, agreed, claiming that had the war continued just another day, "we could have inflicted terrible damage on them."[28] Ending it earlier "did leave some escape routes open for them to get back out." Talabani concurred: "If President Bush had only continued the fighting two more days, Saddam's armed forces would have completely broken down."[29]

As Saddam began to put the Kurdish rebellion down, Talabani and Barzani, the co-presidents of the Kurdish Front, appealed to Bush for help by reminding him: "You personally called upon the Iraqi people to rise up against Saddam Hussein's brutal dictatorship."[30] In addition, Talabani pointed out that "with the approval of the allies a transmitter, 'Voice of Free Iraq,' was set up, which also called for an uprising."[31] (The Kurdish leader was referring to secret orders Bush had given the CIA in January to aid rebels in Iraq with a clandestine, antigovernment radio station.[32])

For a number of reasons, however, the United States chose not to intervene in the internal Iraqi strife. Doing so could lead, it was feared, to an unwanted, protracted American occupation that would be politically unpopular in the United States, to an unstable government in Iraq, or even "Lebanization" of the country and destabilization of the Middle East. What is more, the United States also concluded that Saddam could win. To support the Kurds against him might require an unwanted, perpetual United States commitment. Also, Kurdish success in Iraq might provoke Kurdish uprisings in Turkey, Syria, or Iran, states whose cooperation the United States needed. A U.S. Senate Foreign Relations staff report written by Peter Galbraith and issued a month after Saddam had put down the rebellion confirmed that the United States "continued to see the opposition in caricature" and feared that the Kurds would seek a separate state and that the Shiites wanted an Iranian-style Islamic republic.[33] Another reason was that the United States had fought Iraq to vindicate the principle of Kuwait's territorial integrity without which instability and chaos would reign. To support uprisings that threatened Iraq's territorial integrity would make the United States look hypocritical.

Given these factors, it might almost be concluded that the United States implicitly had returned to its pre-August 1990 policy of seeing Saddam as a source of stability in the volatile region. What is more likely, however, is that the United States was simply reacting on an ad hoc basis to circumstances but certainly did not want Saddam to remain in power. The problem was how to remove him without exceeding what were felt to be the legitimate bounds of intervention.

REFUGEES

The failed rebellion quickly led to a human tragedy of unbelievable proportions. Reports spoke of "hundreds of thousands of Kurds fearing government reprisals . . . fleeing by any means possible into the mountains along the Iranian and Turkish borders, turning roadways into ribbons of humanity."[34] By early May Ahmad Hoseyni, the director general in charge of foreign nationals and immigrants in Iran, announced that "the number of the Iraqi refugees arriving in Iran has surpassed 1.117 million."[35] In late April Hayri Kozakcioglu, the regional governor in the southeast of Turkey, reported "that there are currently around 468,000 northern Iraqis in Turkey's border region with Iraq."[36] These new arrivals joined the 30,000 Iraqi Kurdish refugees remaining in Turkey from the 1988 exodus, which now seemed to pale into insignificance in comparison.

These new refugees threatened to overwhelm their hosts. Indeed, there were some in Turkey who thought the problem was in part Saddam's revenge for that state having supported the allies in the Gulf War: "This is the sneakiest form of aggression and Saddam should not be allowed to get away with it."[37]

In response, Turkish President Ozal called on all countries to join together as they had in that war, adding that "otherwise, a new dispute will be created in the Middle East and that a problem threatening peace and stability will be created."[38] Elaborating, he argued that "even the most perfect organization cannot cope with such an influx within such a short period. . . . It is impossible for any country to solve a problem of such proportions by itself."

What could be done? With the understanding that the settlement of the refugees on or near the Turkish border could only be a temporary expedient, the following possibilities existed. Everything should be done to pressure Baghdad to allow the refugees to return home under guarantees for their safety. As Regional Governor Hayri Kozakcioglu maintained: "The solution to this problem is to be able to send them back to their own homes. All countries of the world should unite and put pressure on the Iraqi Government for the safe return of these people to their own homes."[39] Certainly, Iraq did not want to face a new allied intervention. What is more, Turkey and its U.N. allies could use the economic carrot, since Turkey currently was the only state that could provide an outlet for Iraqi oil.

Massive Western aid was a second possibility. The lack of such a response in 1988, however, did not bode well for this idea. Indeed at that time Turkey not only had to assume most of the refugee burden itself, but it also was subjected to sanctimonious Western criticism for not doing enough. In faulting the initial Western response this time, one Turkish journalist argued that "the amount of the aid these countries have provided to the refugees to date does not even equal that which the people of Turkey's Hakkari province have provided."[40]

Nevertheless, this time, unlike in 1988, the West was more involved in the situation, since it had just fought the war and then encouraged the uprising that had led to the problem. In addition, Turkey's decision to keep most of the refugees on the border, instead of allowing them into the country, may actually have helped the refugees by forcing the West and the United Nations to become more involved.

Would the West have responded as readily to the problem if only Iran had been involved as a host state? Referring to the meager aid his country had received up to that point, Iranian President Hashemi Rafsanjani, declared: "Shame on you. The costs are astronomical, and what you gave is equal to what a single Iranian village has donated. All your mouth-filling titles of human rights, International Red Cross, are lies, all lies."[41] Dr. David M. Reed, a volunteer with the private relief organization Americares, "praised Iran's effort to assist the Kurds, but said that it had been overwhelmed by the exodus of refugees."[42] After Iran finally appealed for international assistance, the European Economic Community responded, while the United States continued to concentrate on the problem in Turkey.

SAFE HAVENS

Initially proposed by Turkish President Ozal and then picked up and advocated by British Prime Minister John Major, the concept of "enclaves," later changed to "safe havens,"[43] in northern Iraq, where the refugees would be protected from being attacked by Saddam's forces, eventually caused the United States and the United Nations partially to reverse their position on interference in postwar, domestic Iraqi strife.

The United States action produced a variety of political and legal problems. Politically it might (1) enmesh the United States in an interminable conflict between Baghdad and the Kurds; (2) result in an embryonic Kurdish state that would act as an unwanted model for the Turkish Kurds; (3) serve as a base for the Kurdish Workers Party (PKK) guerrillas to stage raids on Turkey; and (4) become a second Gaza Strip or home to generations of permanent refugees, stateless, embittered, and, therefore, disruptive.

Legally it was doubtful that the U.N. Security Council would approve such a restriction on Iraqi territorial integrity because of the precedents it might set for the Soviet Union and the Baltic states (which at that time were still not independent) as well as China and Tibet. The United States, in effect, accomplished the functional equivalence, however, by warning Iraq not to use either fixed-wing airplanes or helicopters north of the thirty-sixth parallel, nor to interfere with relief work anywhere in Iraq. By the middle of May, more than 250,000 Kurds had moved into the safe havens, leaving some 180,000 in Turkey; 8,000 United States, British, and French troops occupied the zone, while thousands more were "just over the horizon" in Turkey and the eastern Mediterranean if needed. Kurds who had escaped into Iran, however, returned much slower.

Iraqi Foreign Minister Ahmad Husayn Khudayyir declared that the United States action "constitutes a flagrant interference in the internal affairs of Iraq, an independent country and member of the United Nations,"[44] while Al-Thawrah, the mouthpiece of the Baathist Party, denounced the move as a "precedent the likes of which never existed in the history or relations among countries."[45] Nevertheless, Iraq was in no position to offer overt opposition.

Although many observers might have had legalistic qualms, most still would have agreed that the egregious situation justified some such extraordinary action. As U.S. President George Bush said: "We simply could not allow 500,000 to a million people to die up there in the mountains."[46] What is more, as the victor in the Gulf War, the United States might be deemed to have had residual rights of conquest to take such action. In addition, some argued that the 1948 Convention on the Prevention and Punishment of the Crime of Genocide provided a legal basis. Massoud Barzani was already on record as having described the concept of safe havens as "a great humanitarian gesture and a big step forward."[47]

A possible way out of the legal problem was offered by seeing the U.S. action as a logical extension of U.N. Security Council Resolution 688 of April 5, 1991,[48] which condemned "the repression of the Iraqi civilian population . . . in Kurdish populated areas, the consequences of which threaten international peace and security in the region" and demanded "that Iraq . . . immediately end this repression." It was the first time in its forty-six-year history that the world body had so explicitly addressed the Kurdish question in Iraq. This Resolution was then followed by an agreement signed by the United Nations and Iraq on April 18, to permit the international organization to assume refugee assistance operations in Iraq.[49]

By the middle of July, however, the entire question had become moot because the allied forces had been withdrawn. "A delicate balance of power between Saddam's men in the cities and the Kurds in the hills"[50] had formed. Indeed, by the fall of 1991, as Baghdad consolidated its position by withdrawing its troops southward, the Kurdish Front had reoccupied most of the cities in northern Iraq. The real solution would be to effect an adequate political settlement. Although the negotiations that started between Baghdad and the Kurds in late April constituted a very different approach to the situation, the pressure put on Iraq by the existence of the safe havens may have helped get them started.

♦ ♦ ♦

8

Negotiations

During the height of the refugee crisis in mid-April, Saddam sent
several envoys to Kurdish leaders calling for a "new chapter between the Baghdad government and the Kurds."[1] A "very high-
ranking general" and a Kurd were among those sent. Saddam
probably took this step to at least seem to be trying to solve the Kurdish problem, which was preventing him from even beginning to nor-
malize his rule over Iraq after his shattering defeat in the Gulf War. In
addition, his military victory over the Kurds in March was more apparent than real, since the Kurds still maintained a military presence in
the mountains of the north and were in effect now enjoying a de facto
autonomy behind the cease-fire lines.

Iraqi Foreign Minister Ahmad Husayn Khudayyir announced that
"the proposal from the regime calls for a settlement of the Kurdish problem based on the March 1970 accord concerning the granting of autonomy to the Kurds as well as the realization of pluralism and democracy."
The Kurds accepted "the principle of negotiations," provided that the
Iraqi army stop its attacks on them, a cease-fire be arranged, and all prisoners be released. A KDP spokesman in Damascus said that a cease-fire
then was agreed to on April 16 to permit the leaders of the Kurdistan
Front to study the proposal.[2]

The initial negotiations went through two rounds. Jalal Talabani was
the principal Kurdish representative at the first (April 18-24) and
Massoud Barzani at the second (May 6-18). Each was absent from the
talks the other attended. Only four of the then seven announced members of the Iraqi Kurdistan Front attended both rounds: the KDP, PUK,
SPKI, and KPDP, headed by Sami Rahman. At the first round the SPKI
was represented by its leader, Rasul Mamand; Mahmud Uthamn represented the group during the second round. Nechirvan Idris Barzani
(Massoud's nephew, heir apparent, and already a member of the KDP

leadership) represented his party at the first series of meetings. The other reputed members of the Front were either too insignificant to participate or were kept away by some type of disagreement. For example, although a member of the Front, the Kurdistan Branch of the ICP did not take part because it felt that the talks would strengthen Saddam and weaken the Kurds' international position.[3]

On the Iraqi side, it was first reported that Foreign Minister Khudayyir was representing his government, but later it became clear that Izzat Ibrahim, the vice chairman of Iraqi's ruling Revolutionary Command Council (RCC) and thus probably the number-two man in the ruling hierarchy, actually did so. (Khudayyir may have played this role at first before more substantive discussions began.) In addition, Deputy Prime Minister Tariq Aziz and Interior Minister Ali Hassan al-Majid were among the Iraqi participants. One report indicated that Prime Minister Sadun Hammadi also took part. Upon the successful completion of the first round of talks, Saddam received the leaders of the four participating Kurdish parties and was seen on Baghdad television actually kissing Talabani!

Following this meeting, Talabani announced to the world the substance of the talks.[4] He declared that "effectively Saddam Husayn had agreed to the end of his dictatorship." There would be "free elections for all parties and . . . multiparty life in Iraq." The RCC would be abolished and the Arabization of Iraqi Kurdistan ended. There also would be a general amnesty for all Iraqi prisoners "in principle."

The talks had dealt with four points: "Improving relations, democracy in Iraq, Kurdish national rights, and the country's national unity." The refugees could return to Iraq in safety because "we have received promises from President Saddam Husayn and others that all Iraqi Kurds will be secure." Regarding the U.S. troops in northern Iraq, Talabani said that "as soon as a final agreement is reached, all foreign forces should withdraw." Until then, however, "we do not object to the presence of other forces to protect the refugees." Talabani declared, though, that he would "prefer the presence of UN forces." The overall agreement "provided greater autonomy for the Kurds in northern Iraq . . . based on the implementation of the 11 March 1970 agreement."

Where in this incredible litany of trust and goodwill was there any doubt or hesitation? What would keep Saddam from tearing up any agreement once he had regained his strength? Illustrating that he had not been totally relieved of his senses, the co-president of the Kurdish Front declared that "he wanted further negotiations with the Iraqis on the question of international guarantees for the agreement, which . . .

should come from the United States and the United Nations." He also stated that the issue of Kirkuk, which had bedeviled the two sides in the 1970s, would be discussed "later."

The second round of negotiations—in which Barzani assumed the leading position on the Kurdish side, while Talabani absented himself—seemingly moved the reconciliation process even further. On the two key points of difference Talabani had noted, however—international guarantees and the status of Kirkuk—Barzani's evolving position seemed suspect.

As late as April 23, the leader of the KDP had declared that the Kurds "will not sign any agreement that does not include some international guarantees" and that whatever the talks going on in Baghdad were about, "they must include international guarantees on the refugees."[5] Even when Barzani himself actually began participating in the negotiations, a KDP spokesman affirmed that "international guarantees for an autonomy agreement remain the greatest problem. . . . We have had bitter experience with how those in power in Baghdad keep agreements."[6] The KDP representative also added that "he hopes for a compromise on the Kurds having a share in the income from the oil reserves in the region around Kirkuk."

What instead did Barzani do? In respect to international guarantees, the co-president of the Kurdish Front decided that "at present, I believe that democracy is more important. If there is a new agreement and democracy has been achieved, our people will support it and believe in it. Anyway, we were not a negotiating party on this issue."[7] When then asked how Saddam viewed democracy, Barzani replied cryptically: "His excellency the president has 24 years of experience in government. We believe that this is the best way to serve Iraq, the Ba'th Party, the government, and the Iraqi people." As for a share of the oil in Kirkuk, he announced: "Oil, whether in Karkuk or other areas, belongs to the central government." Barzani did, however, declare that "defining the autonomous region . . . [constituted] the key point which we are trying to resolve with the government."

In regard to the person many would characterize as the archenemy of the Kurds, Barzani now thought that "President Saddam Husayn has spoken about essential points that proved his love for the Kurds, his concern for the Kurdish problem, and the soundness of his treatment of its developments."[8] The Kurdish leader went on to emphasize "that President Saddam Husayn's leadership is the only basic guarantee for the Kurds in any agreement" and that "Saddam . . . reassures us about our demands and rights."

This turn of events was incredible, to say the least. Could Barzani have been trying to signal his own disbelief when he recalled: "Caution and worry . . . [had] permeated the [1970] peace talks, but following a closed meeting between President Saddam Husayn and my father, Mustafa Barzani, the two emerged out from the meeting smiling, and so worry was dissipated and delight overwhelmed the audience." We might agree, saying yes, but what then had occurred?

As for the specifics of their agreement, Barzani made some of the following points.[9] "The 11 March 1970 declaration was the basis of all the ideas being discussed." There would be a general amnesty, return of the Kurds to their homes, repeal of the emergency laws, and opening of a university in Sulaymaniya, as well as other educational and cultural steps for the Kurds. The negotiations on democracy had resulted in six major points: (1) separation of party and government; (2) constitutional legitimacy; (3) political and party pluralism; (4) separation of judicial, executive, and legislative functions; (5) holding of elections; and (6) freedom of the press.

Barzani noted, however, "that no final agreement, so far, had been signed." Indeed, "the government rejected the establishment of a coalition government between the Kurdish political parties and the Iraqi Government." Uthman of the SPKI, who also took part in the news conference, made it clear that the mechanics of drawing up a new constitution for Iraq remained uncertain. In regard to the Kurdish guerrilla fighters, Barzani stated: "The Peshmerga will be part of the Iraqi forces and might become part of the internal security forces. We are part of the Iraqi people and our organization will become part of the Iraqi organizations."

The Kurdish negotiations and apparent agreement with the government called forth angry criticism from the Kurdish Front's erstwhile allies in the Iraqi opposition. Saad Salih Jabr, the chairman of the Free Iraqi Council, cabled Barzani: "We were surprised and shocked . . . by the Kurdish Front's holding of negotiations with Saddam's regime. We were more shocked by the . . . exchanging [of] kisses and embraces with Saddam at a time when the blood of the . . . Iraqi people in general has not yet dried."[10] Jabr then declared that "we have a great hope that you will reconsider your agreement in principle on negotiation and refuse to sign in any way any agreement with the regime."

Similarly an "open appeal from a number of Iraqi opposition leaders" reminded the Kurdish negotiators in Baghdad that "Saddam has breached pledges and agreements."[11] He had only made the present one "in a state of weakness. . . . But as soon as he has the situation under control, he will disavow his pledges and devote his time to carry out mass killings." The "appeal" then went on to declare that "your agreement to negotiate with him [Saddam] . . . troubled and pained us . . . because you are a major partner in the Iraqi opposition." Membership in this group "constitutes a moral and ethical commitment . . . to topple Saddam Husayn and overthrow his regime." Thus, concluded the message, it was hoped "that you stop negotiating with Saddam and his gang, forget the matter, and put your hands once again in the . . . Iraqi opposition."

Muhsin Bizzi, a member of the KDP Political Bureau, and other party officials meeting in London "advised . . . Barzani to take more time and act carefully before signing any agreement with the unreliable regime of the tyrant."[12] Other Iraqi opposition sources described the agreement "as an open door for the tyrant's forces to attack the opposition." Another KDP spokesman "called on the United Nations to provide guarantees for the agreement recently signed in Baghdad." A dispatch from Tehran noted that "the Kurdish leaders who reside abroad, despite the optimistic reports they get through the media . . . still speak with some caution about the achievements of the Baghdad negotiations."[13]

The ICP, which had recognized the legitimacy of Kurdish rights and aspirations since the 1930s, pointed out that three of the members of the Iraqi Kurdish Front had not been present at the negotiations and added "that there is not reason to trust Hussein to keep his word even if a settlement were reached."[14] Ali Reber, a spokesman for the National Liberation Front of Kurdistan (ERNK), an affiliate of the PKK, declared: "It is incomprehensible and irresponsible that now, with Kurds being persecuted and killed by Iraq troops, one should sit down at the table with the regime in Baghdad."[15]

ELUSIVE AGREEMENT

Barzani continued negotiating with the regime in Baghdad until June 16. Then he returned north, claiming that an agreement was in hand: "We have achieved very good results, and I think the matter is finished. . . . I will return to Baghdad in the next few days and the agreement will be signed."[16] Since it was the fruit of the dramatic negotiations conducted both by Barzani and Talabani and also was tentatively endorsed by more than 500 Kurdish elders, it would be useful to cite the text of the proposed "Autonomy Draft Law" in some detail.[17]

In the name of the people, the Revolution Command Council . . . [and] in accordance with the provisions of paragraph A of Article 42 of the

Constitution and with the 11 March 1970 statement, the RCC . . . decided to issue the following law. . . .

Autonomy law for the region of Kurdistan:
Chapter I:

Section 1: The general basis:

Article I
A. The region of Kurdistan will enjoy autonomy and will be referred to as "the region" wherever it is mentioned in this law.
B. The region will be defined as that area where the majority of the population are Kurds, and the general census will confirm the boundaries of the region in accordance with the 11 March statement. The 1957 census regulations will determine the ethnic character of the absolute majority of the population in the areas where a general census is to be held.
C. The region will be considered a corporate administrative unit enjoying autonomy within the framework of the legal, political, and economic unity of the Iraqi Republic. The administrative divisions within it will meet the provisions of the governorates law while taking account of the provisions of this law.
D. Irbil will be the center of the autonomy administration.
E. The autonomy institutions are part of the Iraqi Republic's institutions.

Article 2
A. The Kurdish language is an official language in the region together with the Arabic language.
B. The Arabic and Kurdish languages will be the teaching languages at all stages and in all Kurdish educational establishments in the region. . . .
F. All stages of education in the region will be subject to the general education policy of the state.

Article 3
A. The rights and freedoms of Arab nationals and the minorities in the region are guaranteed under the provisions of the Constitution and relevant laws and decisions. The autonomy administration is committed to guaranteeing the exercise of these rights and freedoms....
C. Arab nationals and members of the minorities in the region will be represented in all the autonomy institutions on the basis of their proportion of the population of the region and will occupy posts in accordance with the laws and decisions regulating them.

Article 4
The judiciary is independent and answerable only to the law. Its formations in the region are an integral part of the judicial structure of the Iraqi republic.

Section 2: The financial basis:

Article 5
The region is an independent financial unit within the state's financial unity.

Article 6
A. The region will have its special budget within the unified overall state budget.
B. The preparation and regulation of the region's budget will be subject to the same rules and principles used in the preparation of the unified overall state budget.

Article 7
The region's budget will comprise the following budgets. . . .

Article 8
The region's budget revenues will be as follows:
1. The intrinsic revenues consisting of the following:
A. Revenues allocated to the region's municipalities and local administrations under the law.
B. Revenues from sales and services of the departments, establishments, and interests administratively and financially linked to the autonomy [region]. . . .
3. A special five-year renewal budget to ensure growth and development of the region in parallel with the rest of the Iraqi Republic.

Article 9
The region's accounts will be subject to the control of the central financial control and audit department.

Chapter II: Autonomy Institutions

Section 1: The legislative council:

Article 10
The legislative council is the legislative body elected by the inhabitants of the region in a general secret direct ballot. . . .

Article 11
A. The legislative council will elect a speaker, deputy speaker, and secretary from its members.
B. The council sessions will be held in the presence of the majority of its members. Its decisions will be based on the majority of those present except where the legislative council law stipulates otherwise.

Article 12
The legislative council will exercise the following powers, within the limits of the constitution and the law:
A. Draw up its own bylaws.

B. Make the legislative decisions necessary for the development of the region in its local social, cultural, constructional, and economic aspects within the confines of the state's general policy.

C. Make legislative decisions relating to the development of the cultural characteristics and national traditions of the region's citizens. . . .

E. Approve the region's development plan and approve the detailed draft plans prepared by the executive council. . . .

F. Approve the region's budget after it has been approved by the executive council, and refer it to the central authorities for consideration.

G. Introduce amendments to the region's budget after its approval. . . .

I. Seek a vote of confidence in the executive council or in one or more of its members. Whoever loses a vote of confidence will be relieved of his duties. The withdrawal of confidence will be based on a majority decision by the legislative council members.

Section 2: The executive council:

Article 13

A. The executive council is the executive body of the autonomy administration in the region.

B. The executive council will comprise its chairman, his deputy, and a number of members equal to the number of secretariats mentioned in article 64 [sic] of this law or exceeding it by two members.

C. The president of the republic will ask one of the legislative council members to act as chairman of and to form the executive council.

D. The designated chairman will choose the members of the executive council and his own deputy from the members of the legislative council or from those who meet membership requirements. He will then go to the legislative council for a vote of confidence. Once a vote of confidence has been won from a majority of the council members, a republican decree will be issued establishing the executive council. . . .

H. By virtue of his post, the chairman of the executive council will be a member of the cabinet. . . .

J. The president of the republic may relieve the executive council chairman of his post, in which case the council will be regarded as dissolved.

Article 14

1. The executive council chairman will be the most senior executive chairman in the region with regard to the autonomy administrations and associated departments, and decisions and orders will be issued in his name.

2. The region's governorates will be linked to the executive council chairman.

3. The following secretariats will be linked to the executive council:

A. Internal affairs, B. Education, C. Housing and reconstruction, D. Agriculture and irrigation, E. Culture, information, and youth, F. Tourism, G. Social and health affairs, H. Economic and financial affairs and light industries, [and] I. Awqaf affairs. . . .

Article 15

1. The executive council will exercise its powers as follows:

A. To guarantee implementation of laws and regulations.

B. To adhere to the judiciary's rulings.

C. To spread justice; maintain security and order; and protect public, national and local amenities and state funds in accordance with the provisions of the present law. . . .

F. To prepare the region's draft general plan and detailed draft economic plans.

G. To supervise local public establishments in the region.

H. To appoint employees of autonomy administrations whose appointment does not require a republic decree or the president of the republic's approval. . . . They will be subject to the provisions of the laws applying to employees of the Iraqi Republic. Employees in the administrative areas inhabited by a Kurdish majority will be Kurds or from among those enjoying a good command of the Kurdish language, taking into account what is mentioned in Article 2 of this law. . . .

K. To implement the region's budget in accordance with the laws and rules approved by the state's accounting system.

L. To prepare an annual report on the region's conditions and to refer it to the president of the republic and the legislative council. . . .

Chapter III: Relationship Between Central Authority and Autonomy Administration:

Article 16

With the exception of the powers exercised by the autonomy bodies, authority throughout the Iraqi republic will be exercised [by] the central bodies or their representatives.

Article 17

1. Police and traffic formations in the region will be linked to their general directorates at the Interior Ministry for the purposes of technical aspects and service affairs. . . .

Article 18

1. Central authority departments in the region will be under the ministries to which they belong and will carry out their work within the boundaries of their own domains, and the competent autonomy bodies will be entitled to express observations to their officials within the framework of coordination and of serving public welfare. . . .

Article 19

1. The president of the republic will be entitled to dissolve the legislative council in the event it is difficult for it to exercise its powers due to the resignation

of half of its members, its failure to secure the legal quorum within 30 days from the date it is called to convene, its failure on more than two successive times to obtain the confidence stipulated by clause 4 of Article 13 of this law, or its failure to comply with the decisions of the control authority stipulated in Chapter IV of this law.

2. In the event of the legislative council's dissolution, the executive council will continue to exercise its powers until the election of the new legislative council within a maximum period of 90 days as of the date the republican decree dissolving it is issued.

Chapter IV: Legitimacy Control [Authority]

Article 20:
1. A body called the "legitimacy control authority" will be set up, comprising seven members, three of whom will be nominated by the speaker of the National Assembly (the Shura council), provided that two of them are jurists. The chairman of the legislative council of the autonomous region will nominate three members, provided that two of them are jurists.

2. The president of the republic will choose the chairman of the legitimacy control authority.

3. The chairman and members of the control authority will be appointed by a republican decree for four years, renewable only once. The authority's chairman or any of its members may not be relieved of his post during the membership term unless he expresses his wish to do so.

Article 21
The control authority will consider the following:
1. The legality of the autonomy bodies' decisions.
2. The extent to which the draft law on amendment of the autonomy law conforms to the provisions of the Constitution and the essence of the autonomy law...
3. Jurisdiction disputes between the central authority and the autonomy bodies.

Article 22
1. The justice minister will be entitled to contest the autonomy bodies' decisions before the control authority for their violation of the Constitution, laws, or regulations. This will be done within 30 days of the date he was informed of them.

2. The chairman of the legislative council of the autonomous region will be entitled to ask the control authority to show the extent to which the draft law on amendment of the autonomy law conforms to the Constitution and the essence of the autonomy law.

3. (A). The competent minister will be entitled to request the control authority to determine the domain of any departments of the autonomy bodies as well as his own ministry's sphere of authority with regard to a particular question.

(B). The executive council chairman will be entitled to request the control authority to determine the sphere of authority of any central authority department or any of the autonomy bodies' departments with regard to a particular question.

Article 23

1. The control authority will examine a contestation submitted to it by the justice minister or the executive council chairman within 30 days of the date the contestation is submitted.

2. The control authority will examine a request submitted to it by the competent minister or the executive council chairman within 30 days of the date the request is submitted to it with regard to determining the sphere of authority.

Article 24

1. A contestation submitted to the control authority by the justice minister against the autonomy bodies' decisions will suspend their implementation until it is decided.

2. Decisions of the autonomy bodies which the control authority decides are illegal will be regarded as invalid in whole . . . or in part as of the date they were issued, and all the legal effects resulting from them will be eliminated.

3. The control authority's decision on the question of determining the sphere of authority will be final and must be implemented.

4. If the control authority decides that the draft law on amendment of the autonomy law violates the provisions of the Constitution or the essence of the autonomy law, its legislative provisions will be suspended. But if the authority discovers that a part of the draft law violates the provisions of the Constitution or the essence of the autonomy law, the authority will remove that part from the draft law. In such a case, its legislation may continue or be disregarded.

5. The control authority will inform the quarters concerned of its decisions, which will be published in the official gazette.

Chapter V: Concluding Provisions

Article 25

This law will not be amended by the National Assembly (and the Shura council) except by a two-thirds majority of its members.

Article 26

The autonomy law of the region of Kurdistan No. 33 of 1974 and its amendments will be abolished, but the regulations and instructions issued under it will remain valid pending their replacement.

Article 27

The Revolution Command Council's decisions on autonomy law No. 33 of 1974 will remain valid without conflicting with the provisions of this law.

Article 28
This law will be implemented as of its date of publication in the official
gazette.

Necessitating Reasons:
Based on the historic statement issued by the Revolution Command Council
on 11 March 1970, which laid the sound foundations for tackling the Kurdish
question on the basis of national unity and historic brotherhood between the
Arabs and the Kurds; and for the sake of developing and enhancing the autonomy experiment represented by law No. 33 of 1974, which continued for 17
years in line with political and economic developments, this law has been
introduced.

Despite Barzani's enthusiasm about the agreement, Talabani cautioned
that the autonomy talks could still "continue for months"[18] and "that he
and the Iraqi refugees do not trust the guarantees that the defeated
tyrant [Saddam] would give if an agreement is reached."[19] After finally
meeting with Barzani in late June, Talabani declared that an agreement
could be signed "only after certain problems are resolved related to the
establishment of a unitary state in Iraq and the joint use of Karkuk city
and Iraqi oil."[20]

Sami Abd al-Rahman, the leader of the KPDP, emphasized "important points which are still suspended, including the determination of the
autonomous region . . . [and] the question of protecting security in the
region—a task that we believe the autonomy authority should be in
charge of."[21] He also argued that "Barzani's optimism was encouraged
by the government with a view to creating an embarrassing atmosphere
for the allies and the United Nations." Uthman of the SPKI shared these
concerns: "Twenty years of struggle against Baghdad have taught the
Front to be very careful regarding Baghdad's attitudes."[22] Illustrative of
the Iraqi government's implicit fears, on the other hand, Saddam told
former Turkish Prime Minister Bulent Ecevit: "The insistence on
Karkuk's inclusion in the autonomous region is indicative of the wish for
separation."[23]

The main problem that made an agreement elusive, however, was not
the "Draft Law on Autonomy" but Saddam's demand that the Kurds
give him "something in return."[24] This six-point requirement took the
form of an appendix Baghdad added to the "Draft Law" entitled the
"Kurdistan Front's Commitments Toward the Homeland."

1. All the armed formations and militias belonging to the Kurdistan Front will be disbanded and all their arms will be handed over to the central authorities within a month of the agreement's announcement.

2. [The Kurds are] to hand over to the state the radio stations owned by the Kurdistan Front once the suspension of transmissions is announced.

3. [The Kurds are] to cease any cooperation or contacts with states inside and outside the region. The same applies to dealings with non-Iraqi parties and their members. As for friendly parties, the method of contacting them and establishing relations with them can be determined through the frontal [jabhawi] action charter to be agreed.

4. Iraq has suffered, and still suffers, serious threats to its national and strategic security—first and foremost, the Zionist-imperialist threat and the regime in Iran. In order for the national response to these threats to be at the required level, the Kurdistan Front will be committed to the plans and measures taken by the Iraqi state to achieve this noble national objective, whether through the military fighting method or the nationalist political struggle. It will also be committed to developing the masses' awareness with regard to love for the homeland and readiness to defend it until martyrdom.

5. [The Kurds will support the Baath Party] in order to confront the artificial religious or nationalistic political groups that threaten Iraq's strategic security because of their links with foreign forces.

6. The Kurdistan Front [will] be fully committed to implementing a central national program drawn up by the Ba'th Party and the Kurdish Front and designed to spread correct national awareness and to create a spirit of discipline, commitment, and respect for the laws and regulations issued by the state and its organs.

Meeting at its headquarters in Shaqlawa, the Kurdish Front found these demands "unacceptable," since they would require the Kurds to "sever relations with the outside world, lay down their arms, and depend on the Iraqi regime in the political, military, and cultural fields."[25] Dismantling the peshmergas would constitute "a fatal blow to the Kurds, since it would facilitate their liquidation at a later stage."[26] Mahmud Uthman added that security was "very important, and we must not agree to its remaining in the hands of the [Baghdad] security and intelligence organs, which are all controlled by Saddam's relatives."[27] The demands were "humiliating for the Kurds," since they obliged them "not only to abandon their Iraqi allies but to fight them with weapons as well."[28] A PUK spokesman concluded, therefore, that, concerning Saddam's demands, "no government in Iraq has ever obtained them from the Kurds."[29] Commenting on the impasse that had been reached, Rahman added: "First they make you trust them, and when they think that you are sure, they surprise you by requesting such commitments."[30]

IMPASSE

On July 6 in Arbil the Kurdish Front presented a six-point counter-proposal to the Iraqi government. This reply concerned (1) the future status of Kirkuk, (2) democracy in Iraq, (3) security in Iraqi Kurdistan, (4) the surrender of Kurdish heavy weapons, (5) the silencing of Kurdish radio stations, and (6) the termination of Kurdish contacts abroad. It was received coolly. ·

Barzani, Talabani, Uthman, and Rahman represented the Front, while Izzat Ibrahim, Tariq Aziz, and Husayn Kamil spoke for Baghdad. Adding a sense of urgency to the proceedings were the widespread demonstrations against Saddam that occurred in the city just before the two sides met.

After a short break, the negotiations were resumed in Baghdad. Before arriving there, however, Barzani and Talabani took the unusual step of signing an accord on what "minimum demands" they would accept in an attempt to prevent any disagreement between themselves.

Initially, there still seemed some hope. Talabani met personally with Saddam on July 11 and reported that their encounter "was cordial, frank, and very positive."[31] The Kurdish leader was quoted as believing "that an announcement on an autonomous rule agreement is imminent."[32]

However, even if Talabani really felt that this was true, he did not remain in Baghdad to participate in the process. Announcing that Barzani was "fully authorized to complete the dialogue with the government delegation,"[33] Talabani embarked on a seven-nation journey, returning to Iraqi Kurdistan only in mid-August. In reality, the PUK leader probably was reluctant to associate himself any more with the unsuccessful negotiation process, opting instead to solicit support abroad for the next phase of the struggle. Barzani was left to deal with the no-win situation as best as he could.

At first the KDP leader asserted that the final agreement "has been completed and will be announced within a short time."[34] He even went so far as to claim that "foreign hands"[35] had fomented the riots that had broken out between Kurds and the Iraqi army in Sulaymaniya and Arbil on July 18 and earlier. In reality, of course, these increasing incidents were the result of the impasse reached in the negotiations. Indeed, some even argued that the Kurds, who feared that the allies would withdraw, "tried to activate a situation which would make the allied forces come back into Northern Iraq."[36] Barzani was reduced to speculating "on the possibility of achieving democracy in Iraq" in the following nonsensical manner: "We understand the role of the Arab Socialist Ba'th Party. When parties manage to play their roles, and when there is a multiparty system, that will be a great change for us."[37]

A spokesman for the PUK revealed by mid-July that the hopes concerning an agreement "have completely evaporated and negotiations will be difficult and long from now on."[38] Saddam's demand that the Baathists maintain their predominant position was said to be the main reason for this situation. A senior spokesman for the Kurdish Front in Damascus declared that "the Iraqi regime is not prepared to accept the Kurdish plan for democracy, civil rights, the constitution and autonomy" and noted that the "Iraqi authorities had refused to approve political parties . . . motivated by religious confession, region or race."[39]

Other points of disagreement included "the regime's insistence that the Yazidis are Arabs, not Kurds" and Baghdad's rejection of "the establishment of a new Kurdish governorate combining the Kurdish districts of Khanaqin and Klar and their environs, where the majority of the population is Kurdish."[40] According to Mahmud Uthman, "the question of Karkuk is the most important matter being discussed. . . . The Iraqi Government has been reluctant to recognize the rights of the Kurds."[41]

Finally, on August 20, Barzani left Baghdad and returned to his headquarters in the north. Muzaffer Aslan, the secretary-general of the National Turkoman Party of Iraq, reported that he had spoken with representatives of Barzani and Talabani, and "it seems they have lost all hope of reaching an agreement."[42] The senior spokesman for the Kurdish Front in Damascus cited earlier, declared that the negotiations "have reached a dead end."[43]

Amid reports of renewed clashes in Kirkuk and Arbil and a bitter denunciation of Baghdad's continuing policy of Arabization in Kirkuk, Talabani asserted: "I believe that not even the deadliest enemy of the Arabs has committed treason and crimes against the Arab nation such as the ones committed by the Ba'th Party."[44] It was a far cry from the PUK leader's flattering comments about Saddam only a month earlier in Baghdad.

As of the fall of 1991, it was apparent that Talabani and Barzani disagreed on how to proceed. The PUK leader thought that the Kurds should not sign any agreement until they were offered a better deal and/or Saddam fell. The secretary-general of the KDP, on the other hand, was tempted to take what was proffered because he thought that the Kurds needed protection now and doubted the West's ability to provide it in the long run. Although Barzani and then Rahman again journeyed to Baghdad to speak with Saddam and other officials in early December, the impasse remained. Indeed, at the end of the year new

Kurdish refugees began to flee from low-intensity but escalating fighting. Given the inability of either side to break the deadlock, an indeterminate but precarious period of no war, no peace had descended on them.

TURKISH INTERVENTION

At the same time as the Kurdish negotiations with Baghdad were reaching an impasse, another event occurred that illustrated the vacuum of Iraqi governmental authority that had arisen in northern Iraq along parts of the Turkish border and the willingness of the Iraqi Kurds to support a foreign government against Baghdad.

It will be recalled that on several occasions in the 1980s, Turkish forces—with the consent of Iraq—crossed the border in pursuit of PKK guerrillas who had been raiding southeastern Turkey from their camps in northern Iraq. (See Chapter 6.) This time, in response to a PKK attack on August 4 that killed nine soldiers at the Samanli gendarme border station in Hakkari province as well as numerous, earlier provocations, Turkey launched, on the following day, large-scale land and air operations into the Ari, Kaniras, and Durji districts of northern Iraq near where the Turkish, Iraqi, and Iranian borders converge. Thus the incursion was well east of the area in which the allies earlier had established safe havens. In contrast to previous operations, this one had the tacit approval of the KDP and PUK, but not Baghdad.

Some 2,000 Turkish commandos, supported by more than 130 air sorties, penetrated ten to twenty miles across the border, destroyed several PKK camps, killed a number of guerrillas, and captured caches of weapons. They met occasional pockets of heavy resistance and even encountered intensive antiaircraft fire in the western part of Durji. Illustrative of the vacuum of Iraqi authority in that area, the Turks claimed that "it is normal that the Iraqi Government should not be given any information about military operations north of 36 degrees north latitude."[45]

Both Talabani and Barzani were warned about the operation beforehand so that they could get any of their partisans out of the area. Neither man was enthusiastic about the operation, and they influenced the Turks to scale it down and terminate it earlier than originally intended. Yet the fact that the two Iraqi Kurdish leaders tacitly supported the Turkish incursion further illustrated their willingness to support a foreign power against Baghdad as well as Iraq's inability to exercise its authority in the area. Mohsin Dizai, a spokesman for Barzani, explained: "We have no objection to this operation at all,"[46] while Talabani declared that "both he and Barzani agreed that Turkey had every right to ensure its national security."[47] The PUK leader did add, however, that "we do not prefer that Turkey retaliates this way to maintain its security."[48]

Osman Ocalan, the brother of the PKK's leader Abdullah (Apo) Ocalan, reacted bitterly to Barzani's and Talabani's position: "What they did was not correct. . . . They gave the green light to Turkey to attack."[49] The younger Ocalan then went on to question the very support Barzani and Talabani had among their followers, a theme the senior Ocalan had touched upon earlier that summer when criticizing the negotiations between them and Baghdad: "These organizations and leadership, which have little support among the people, are . . . a narrowly based clique."[50]

Although acrimony between the PKK and the Iraqi Kurdistan Front might be expected, continued division among the Iraqi Kurds was not. Nevertheless, Mahmud Uthman clearly opposed the pro-Turkish position of his colleagues in the Front when he sarcastically declared: "The Turkish officials have asked us to protect them against the PKK attacks. Are we Turkey's and Ozal's border police?"[51] Hinting at even deeper divisions, Uthman added that "any party within the framework of the Kurdish Front would stand to lose if it moves to agree to act as Turkey's police units. This applies to all the parties in the Kurdish Front."[52]

In October 1991 Turkish forces struck PKK formations in northern Iraq on two more occasions. These new attacks threatened to break the developing relationship between Turkey and the Iraqi Kurds, as Barzani declared that there had been civilian Iraqi casualties and warned that he would oppose further such incursions: "We consider this aggression a declaration of war. Therefore, we will do what we can, and the Turkish regime will be responsible."[53]

However, the tacit Turkish-Iraqi Kurdish alliance continued to hold. Indeed, Suleyman Demirel's return to power, as a result of the national elections that took place in Turkey at the end of 1991, seemed to further it. The new Turkish prime minister even declared, to the approval of the Kurdish Front: "We have to say to Iraq that if you opt for savagery you will find yourself face to face with us. . . . Not being insensitive to the preservation of the Kurdish entity in Iraq is Turkey's new policy."[54]

◆ ◆ ◆

9

United Nations Peacekeeping

hapter VII of the Charter of the United Nations established a rather detailed system of collective security "to confront would-be aggressors, whoever they might be and wherever they might venture to strike, with an overwhelming collection of restraining power assembled by the mass of states in accordance with clear and firm obligations accepted and proclaimed in advance."[1] In other words, whenever aggression would occur, all the other states automatically would come to the aid of the intended victim. This aid would be overwhelming since it would involve all the rest of the states in the world. The knowledge that this aid was automatic and overwhelming would in most cases deter aggression in the first place and certainly defeat it if it actually occurred.

The Cold War, of course, robbed collective security of its necessary attributes of being certain and therefore always overwhelming, since any one of the five permanent members of the Security Council could block a collective security operation by vetoing it. In addition, a number of other problems existed that in practice made true applications of collective security highly unlikely.[2] As Inis Claude, Jr., has written: "the good politician is required to betray the democratic ideal of doing what the people want, the shrewd politician is required to violate his vote-getting instincts, and the wise statesman is required to follow the rule book in a manner befitting an automaton."[3] It did not make much sense for the British and French to go to war against the Soviet Union when that state invaded Finland at the start of World War II, for example, because the real enemy, Nazi Germany, could only gain by such an action. Yet a literal application of the doctrine of collective security demanded just that.

For these reasons and others, therefore, true collective security never worked and probably never would. Rather than simply give up, however, the United Nations, under the leadership of Secretary-General Dag

Hammarskjold in the 1950s, began to develop a more modest but there-fore perhaps more practical alternative, which has come to be known as "peacekeeping": "UN political-military control of local conflict by politically impartial, essentially noncoercive methods."[4]

In peacekeeping, the objective is not to defeat an aggressor (there is no identified aggressor) but to prevent fighting, act as a buffer, keep order, or maintain a cease-fire. In collective security, on the other hand, the object, of course, is to defeat an aggressor. Whereas collective security postulates a two-world situation of an aggressor versus an overwhelming defender, peacekeeping operates in a three-world situation: the two disputants and the neutral peacekeepers.

Peacekeeping forces must be neutral toward the disputants, present with their consent,[5] and usually supplied by the small and medium-size states, not the great powers, as is the case with collective security.[6] Although criticized by some as a mere "Band-Aid-type" operation that simply perpetuates festering conflicts, peacekeeping—sometimes referred to as "Chapter VI and One-Half" of the U.N. Charter because it is more than Chapter VI (peaceful settlement), but less than Chapter VII (collective security)—has come to be hailed as one of the greatest achievements of the United Nations. In 1988, for example, the U.N. peacekeeping forces were presented the Nobel Peace prize. When the Kurdish tragedy began to unfold in April 1991, the U.N.'s peacekeeping experience suddenly became relevant to the situation.

THE UNITED NATIONS BEGINS TO MOVE

As early as January 30, 1991, U.N. Secretary-General Javier Perez de Cuellar declared that "contingency plans for a possible UN observer and peace-keeping role in the Persian Gulf area were being formulated, and that he was studying a Nordic proposal regarding troop contribution to such a body."[7] At that time, of course, no one knew what would occur. On April 2, once the refugee tide had begun, the secretary-general "expressed his grave concern" and "urged maximum restraint and a peaceful resolution of the situation."[8]

This was followed by the unprecedented U.N. Security Resolution 688 of April 5, 1991,[9] which condemned "the repression of the Iraqi civilian population . . . in Kurdish populated areas, the consequences of which threaten international peace and security in the region" and demanded "that Iraq . . . immediately end this repression." The Resolution also insisted "that Iraq allow immediate access by international humanitarian organizations to all those in need of assistance in all parts of Iraq" and requested that "the Secretary-General . . . use all the resources at his disposal, including those of the relevant United Nations agencies, to address urgently the critical needs of the refugees." As mentioned in Chapter 7, it was the first time in its forty-six-year history that the world body had so explicitly addressed the Kurdish question in Iraq.

In reply, Iraq maintained that "saboteurs . . . had penetrated its borders . . . and, through terror and intimidation, convinced many citizens to leave the country."[10] A general amnesty had been declared, and all Iraqi citizens were free to return.

On April 9 the secretary-general appointed Sadruddin Aga Khan as his "Executive Delegate for a United Nations Inter-Agency Humanitarian Programme for Iraq, Kuwait, and the Iraq/Turkey and Iraq/Iran Border Areas."[11] In time, this program came to cover "the work of eight United Nations agencies, 18 non-governmental agencies, and a contingent of 500 United Nations guards. In total, approximately 1,000 international staff serve[d] in Iraq under this programme."[12]

Eric Suy, the secretary-general's personal representative, and then Sadruddin Aga Khan journeyed to Baghdad, where they held talks with the Iraqi authorities. (Sadako Ogata, the U.N. High Commissioner for Refugees, also visited the area on a separate mission.) On April 18 the executive delegate signed a "Memorandum of Understanding," which, in effect, permitted the United Nations to replace the allied efforts in the safe havens by authorizing U.N. humanitarian operations.

Under the terms of this Memorandum:

> Iraq agrees to cooperate with the United Nations to have a humanitarian presence in Iraq, wherever such presence may be needed, and to facilitate it through the adoption of all necessary measures. This shall be ensured through the establishment of United Nations sub-offices and Humanitarian Centres (UNHUCs), in agreement and cooperation with . . . Iraq.
>
> Each Centre will be staffed by United Nations civilian personnel which, in addition to the regular staff members of the relevant United Nations agencies, may also include staff co-opted from the non-governmental organizations, the International Committee of the Red Cross and the League of Red Cross and Red Crescent Societies. . . .
>
> Routes of return, with relay stations along the way as well as logistic back-up capabilities, will be set up urgently in cooperation with the Iraqi authorities to provide to civilians, particularly the women and children as well as the aged and the sick going back to their home areas, the food aid, shelter and basic health care they will need along the way. United Nations staff will accompany such groups, as required.
>
> The United Nations shall take urgent measures, in cooperation with . . . Iraq, for the early stationing of staff as well as the provision of assistance and

relief in all designated centres and, as a matter of priority, those close to the Iraqi borders with its neighbouring countries. For this purpose, the United Nations may, in agreement and cooperation with . . . Iraq, organize air lifts to the areas concerned, as required, as well as transportation by road of humanitarian assistance and relief goods from and through the neighbouring countries under United Nations or other humanitarian auspices. . . . Iraq shall adopt the necessary measures in order to render such aid in a speedy and effective manner.

All Iraqi officials concerned, including the military, will facilitate the safe passage of emergency relief commodities throughout the country. Iraq shall cooperate in granting United Nations field staff access to the parts of the country requiring relief by air or road as needed, to facilitate the implementation and monitoring of the Programme.[13]

Subsequently, a further agreement was reached on May 25 regarding the deployment of a U.N. Guard Contingent and added as an annex to the original Memorandum of April 18. The purpose of these "Blue Guards" was to enhance the security of the U.N. humanitarian operation and be present as "moral witnesses" inspiring confidence in what was transpiring.

In addition to transit camps in the Zakho plain, transit centres/zones (which can best be described as strengthened and enlarged humanitarian centres) will be established along communications routes in other areas of Iraq, wherever such presence may be needed, in agreement with . . . Iraq. United Nations Guards will be assigned as needed to any transit centres, United Nations sub-offices and Humanitarian Centres (UNHUCs) which may be established by the United Nations in Iraq.

The number of Guards in the Contingent will be kept under review as further units are dispatched, but will not exceed a total strength of 500. In order to ensure their mobility, special arrangements will be made to import the required number of suitable vehicles. Arrangements will be made to ensure that United Nations-marked helicopter(s) will be allowed to land in Dohuk, Zakho and Mosul, as well as in the other areas, for the movement of United Nations personnel. Necessary arrangements will also be made to provide the Contingent with the required means of communication and the necessary logistical back-up.

The number of Guards assigned to the various regions will be decided in consultation with the Government authorities concerned, but would not exceed 150 in any one region. They will move freely, as their duties require, between humanitarian reception points, transit centres and relay stations, as well as sub-offices, using appropriate existing accommodation facilities in the provincial capitals, other towns and villages, or ad hoc field accommodation at transit centres.

United Nations Guards will be authorized to carry side-arms (pistols/revolvers), which will be provided by the Iraqi authorities (subject to the approval of the United Nations with respect to make, model, calibre and munitions). While it is not anticipated that all Guards will be so armed, United Nations guidelines and practices will be followed in this regard.

The Iraqi authorities will appoint a Chief Liaison Officer to facilitate the Contingent's operations and a liaison officer at each centre to facilitate their work with the authorities. The Iraqi authorities will grant appropriate facilities in Baghdad and elsewhere, including office space, maintenance and repair support, maps, etc.[14]

IMPLEMENTATION

The U.N. humanitarian operation in northern Iraq began to be implemented in May 1991 and was in full swing by June. The allied forces turned over the assistance program they had established to the U.N. High Commissioner for Refugees (UNHCR) on June 7. By the middle of July, the last allied troops were out of the area, although Operation Poised Hammer, stationed north of the border in Diyarbakir, Turkey, continued to provide an allied air deterrent against renewed Iraqi aggression against the Kurds.

Refugees and Repatriation

According to the U.N. secretary-general, initially "the main objective was to sustain and support the refugees until they could return home."[15] Once this was accomplished by June, the activities of UNHCR were focused primarily on repatriation protection and the implementation of short-term sanitation and water projects. Working in close cooperation with other U.N. agencies such as the Office of the Executive Delegate, World Food Program (WFP), World Health Organization (WHO), United Nations Children's Fund (UNICEF), International Organization for Migration (IOM) as well as various nongovernmental organizations, UNHCR successfully assisted the reintegration of the returning population. By October it had begun a winterization program to provide shelter for needy civilians in the northern governorates of Dohuk, Arbil, and Sulaymaniya.

WHO sent technical missions to assess the health needs of the some half-million Kurds who had fled to Turkey. These teams operated along the Iraqi-Turkish border by organizing training courses in emergency relief operations for the local staff and coordinating the health component of the U.N. operations. After the refugees were sent home and the

Turkish camps were emptied, the priority shifted to areas within Iraq and Iran.

To provide for the refugees' most immediate needs, UNHCR developed and distributed a basic relief package consisting of jerry cans, cooking sets, water buckets, and soap. Tents, blankets, and plastic sheeting were also distributed to those lacking any other form of shelter.

To guarantee clean water supplies, generators, pumps, and pipes were purchased and installed in at least fifty villages. UNHCR also conducted nutritional surveys and provided basic and emergency health kits for clinics to supplement UNICEF and WHO supplies.

UNICEF provided over 8 million sachets of oral rehydration salts to health centers and hospitals throughout Iraq to help control diarrheal diseases and conducted workshops on the subject in various governorates for health workers. A related top priority was the emergency provision of essential drugs. In addition, UNICEF distributed approximately 275 basic emergency health kits, each of which could aid 10,000 people for three months. More than 1,000 tons of medical supplies were given out.

Some eighty U.N. volunteers (UNV) specialists were particularly effective in quickly providing crucially needed manpower in the initial stages of the various humanitarian programs. Most of them served in Iraq itself as well as Iran, Syria, and Jordan working with WFP, UNICEF, UNHCR, IOM, WHO, and the Iraq Relief Coordination Unit (IRCU). In all, the UNV specialists provided 273 man-months of work.

U.N. Guards Contingent

The U.N. Guards Contingent in Iraq (UNGCI) "was crucial in ensuring the successful handover of humanitarian operations in the north from the coalition forces to the United Nations and in the subsequent establishment of a 'climate of security' in northern Iraq."[16] As of October 1991, its complement of 500 authorized guards, representing thirty-five different nationalities, was in place.

The U.N Guards are composed of a headquarters in Baghdad and four sectors in the north and south of Iraq. Each is divided into sectoral headquarters and subsectors to which staff are assigned on a rotational basis. The office in Baghdad consists of ten guards and includes the operations, administration/logistic support, and movement control units. In northern Iraq, guards are stationed in three different sectors: (1) Sulaymaniya (Raniya, Said Sadiq and Kalar subsectors), (2) Arbil (Sadiq subsector), and (3) Dohuk (Amadia and Zakho subsectors).

These U.N. Guards provide protection to the staff of the entire inter-agency humanitarian program; to U.N. property, warehouses, and offices; and later to the 1,500 trucks in UNHCR's winterization convoys. Patrols are carried out on a twenty-four-hour basis covering some 400,000 kilometers. In addition, the Guards are supposed to report on any incident that might affect the security situation and the effective implementation of the humanitarian program. On a number of occasions, they have helped to prevent clashes and the possible loss of life. In carrying out this role, they also "assure the continued attention of the international community and constitute an element of stability in a volatile situation. Indeed, their presence furnishes a form of 'moral testimony.'"[17]

Finances

Financing has often been a serious problem for U.N. peacekeeping operations. Indeed the United Nations Congo Operation (ONUC) (1960-1964) virtually bankrupted the world organization and led to a serious constitutional crisis over the payment of U.N. dues.[18]

Even before the flood of Kurdish refugees began in April 1991, however, the United Nations had developed a Regional Action Plan to move adequate supplies into the Gulf area, upgrade and expand camp sites, and provide a management system in Jordan, Syria, Turkey, and Iran.[19] Both the United Nations Disaster Relief Organization (UNDRO) and the International Committee of the Red Cross (ICRC) issued funding appeals—the former for $175 million and the latter for $112—on the assumption that there might be as many as 400,000 refugees. Only $136 million was pledged to both appeals, however, because the refugee flow was very light when the war first ended. Nevertheless, some relief infrastructure was already in place in Turkey and Iran as the tide began.

A new U.N. appeal issued on April 5 had to be revised dramatically upward by April 9. A May appeal, updated in June to include the U.N. Guards Contingent, requested $460.3 million, $285.6 million of which had been received as of October 29, 1991.[20]

On August 15 the U.N. Security Council adopted Resolution 706, which permitted Iraq to sale $1.6 billion worth of petroleum, approximately two-thirds of which would go toward providing humanitarian aid within the country. Saddam's regime, however, refused to cooperate on the grounds that the plan encroached upon its sovereignty. Early in January 1992 it was announced that the United Nations and its affiliated agencies had provided approximately $300 million in humanitarian assistance to the entire Gulf region since March 1991.[21] On January 8, 1992, the United Nations issued a new appeal for $145 million to fund operations through June. Obviously there was a shortage of funds.

Continuation

On November 24, 1991, the U.N. peacekeeping mission in northern Iraq was extended for another six months to cover the period January 1-June 30, 1992. This new Memorandum of Understanding continued the framework for U.N. humanitarian activities, primarily the provision of food, medical care, and shelter conducted through centers staffed by U.N. personnel. The Memorandum also provided for maintaining the 500 U.N. Guards to protect U.N. personnel, assets, and operations as well as to help deter violence between the Iraqi army and the Kurdish peshmergas.

At the end of 1991, Saddrudin Aga Khan resigned as the executive delegate of the secretary-general. With the successful return of the refugees, the UNHCR was no longer needed as the lead U.N. agency. The United Nations Development Program (UNDP) or UNICEF was to assume this role.

There had been problems, however. In October 1991 renewed fighting broke out between the Iraqi forces and the Kurds. This caused thousands of Kurds to be dislocated just as winter was approaching. Baghdad's ensuing blockade curtailed the distribution of needed food and medical supplies. According to one report the Iraqi government has accused international aid workers of gathering intelligence.

A U.N. proposal to open new humanitarian centers in Kirkuk and Nasiriya in the south was rejected despite some 250,000 refugees being located near these two cities. Nevertheless, despite these problems, the U.N. effort, including the Guards Contingent, continued on a lower level after the Memorandum formally expired at the end of June 1992.[22]

CONCLUSIONS

The imperfect but effective U.N. collective security operation against Iraq following that state's conquest of Kuwait in August 1990 eventually led to an equally flawed, but still useful peacekeeping operation to help save the Kurds from Saddam's further depredations after their failed uprising in March 1991. At a time when many were hailing the new effectiveness of the United Nations, it is ironic that the world organization was forced into this peacekeeping operation only because the supposedly defeated Saddam was still able to triumph over the Kurds and then force them into a deadly flight to the mountains on the Iranian and Turkish borders.

The United Nations's response proved to be a unique peacekeeping operation because, in effect, it was taking the side of the Iraqi Kurds and the allies against Iraq. This situation patently contrasted with the criterion of impartiality previous peacekeeping operations had developed.

What is more, for the first time, the United Nations had declared in Security Council Resolution 688 of April 5, 1991, that "the repression of the Iraqi civilian population, including most recently, Kurdish populated areas" could "threaten international peace and security." In other words, the Council was saying that circumstances may arise in which extraordinary humanitarian needs would compel the world organization to intervene in the internal affairs of a sovereign state under the collective-security provisions of U.N. Charter Chapter VII. If so, this was certainly a precedent-setting declaration.

Previously, what a state did to its own minorities was of little or no concern to outsiders. Again, therefore, the U.N. peacekeeping operation in northern Iraq carried major implications for the future of international law and organization.

On the other hand, the Kurdish peacekeeping operation was not only low-key and ad hoc, but clearly secondary to and, in effect, part of the allies' political and military operations against Iraq both before and after the Gulf War. Nevertheless, as the secretary-general himself noted:

> A number of precedents were established which might well be of interest for future humanitarian efforts: the decision to aid the direct return of refugees to their homelands via a system of "blue routes," thereby avoiding the need to construct and administer refugee camps; the creation . . . of a United Nations guards contingent to protect United Nations personnel and property, to provide an element of security and stability and to serve as "moral witness" in the humanitarian sphere; and the development of a system whereby a country with sufficient resources could assume responsibility for the care of the vulnerable groups within its borders.[23]

Perhaps the most immediate result of the initial allied effort followed by the U.N. peacekeeping operation was how quickly so many refugees returned to their homes. During April and May 1991, under some of the most despicable conditions imaginable, approximately 1.5 million Kurds had fled to Iran and another 450,000 to Turkey. By the end of August, however, all but 124,300 of them had returned, "most of them utilizing the systems of humanitarian relief centres (UNHUCS), mobile stations, and blue routes designed and implemented by the United Nations, and encouraged by the 'moral witness' and stability provided by the United nations guards."[24] As the secretary-general concluded: "Given the traditional plight of refugees throughout the world, who may spend years— even decades—in refugee camps far from their homes, this early, voluntary return was a major achievement."

◆ ◆ ◆

10

De Facto Statehood

During the first half of 1992, the Iraqi Kurds began increasingly to move toward the creation of a de facto government in northern Iraq behind the protection of the allied Poised Hammer forces stationed in southeastern Turkey and the U.N. peacekeeping operation discussed in Chapter 9. As Jalal Talabani put it: "Saddam Husayn's aggression against Kuwait . . . led to the emergence of a situation in Iraq which we exploited to establish a free local administration [because] none of the region's states can allow the Iraqi regime to launch a new aggression against Kurdistan."[1]

The economic blockade Baghdad had been imposing on the Kurds since October 23, 1991, along with the withdrawal of government officials from that area ironically had the effect of hardening rather than weakening Kurdish resolve. Whether they wanted to or not, the Kurds were being forced to establish their own de facto government and state to survive. In February and March 1992, for example, Massoud Barzani travelled through Europe to inform various governments of the Kurdish point of view. In Turkey he "held useful and positive talks"[2] with President Turgut Ozal, Prime Minister Suleyman Demirel, Deputy Prime Minister Erdal Inonu, Foreign Minister Hikmet Cetin, and other foreign ministry officials. These talks addressed the general political and economic situation in northern Iraq and bilateral ties between the two sides. A few days later Barzani met in France with Bernard Kouchner, the French secretary of state for humanitarian action and denounced the Iraqi blockade. A day later he met with Roland Dumas, the French foreign minister.

THE ANFAL OPERATION

These trends toward creating a de facto Kurdish state were reinforced by the new revelations concerning the Anfal operation, "the officially administered mass murder of . . . at least 100,000 noncombatant Kurds, perhaps more, beginning no later than February 1988 and ending sometime in September of that same year."[3]

The term "Anfal" comes from the Koran, where it is the title of the eighth sura (chapter) and means "spoils of battle." Muslims believe that God gave this revelation to the Prophet Muhammad so that the laws governing booty in battle would be well defined. By naming the operation "Anfal," the Iraqis were providing a religious justification for the Kurds' slaughter.

Secret Iraqi government documents seized by the Kurds during their March 1991 uprising revealed the essentials of the Anfal operation: "demolished villages, transfer points, poison gas, firing squads, mass graves."[4] Given the unsettled conditions still prevailing in northern Iraq, however, the cables, files, transcripts, and other papers documenting the Anfal campaign have not yet been properly collected or analyzed. Each one of the eight parties in the Kurdish Front reportedly has its own cache of papers.

According to the captured documents, of which Kurdish leaders claim there are "tons, truckloads,"[5] "a Kurd might be arrested for belonging to one of the Kurdish political parties, or for being overheard by an informer to be criticizing Iraqi President Saddam Hussein, or for aiding the enemy during the Iran-Iraq war."[6]

Handwritten lists number "eliminated villages" whose inhabitants are referred to as the "lost ones of the Anfal." Almost certainly, they are dead, probably buried in mass graves dug in southwestern Iraq. A typical example printed on presidential stationery and marked "secret and personal" relates how "2,532 people and 1,869 families" were "captured" during "a heroic Anfal operation" and sent to a "camp." Their fate was described in crude Tikriti slang by Ali Hassan al-Majid, Saddam's cousin and at that time defense minister: "Taking care of them means burying them with bulldozers. That's what taking care of them means."[7] Given revelations such as these, it is not surprising that, to many Kurds, the Baghdad regime had lost its moral right to rule them.

ELECTIONS

Early in 1992, a report on the situation in northern Iraq found that "the remnants of Iraqi civil authority in this region, deprived of leadership and money from Baghdad but lacking direction from any central Kurdish authority, are nearly paralyzed."[8] Thieves steal food stocks and vehicles; corrupt Kurdish officials carry anything they can over the frontier to sell in Iran. Local militia commanders run their areas as personal fiefs. Each member of the Kurdish Front exercises a veto power, with the result that "few decisions are made." Barzani himself admitted: "Some local commanders have misused their power. There have been problems with corruption, especially at the local level. We all realized that we must clean up our ranks." Then he added: "Our governing process is paralyzed."

Dr. Mohammed Bajallan, a plastic surgeon, agreed: "The situation is becoming unbearable. People have nothing to eat and some are willing to kill now for money or food." Dr. Mohammed Gaza Noori, the director of the Sulaymaniya Teaching Hospital, declared that "anarchy and uncertainty" had gripped the region. Cigarette factories in Arbil and Sulaymaniya lay idle because a local leader had commandeered a warehouse full of filters and was attempting to sell them in Iran. When he tried to intervene, a PUK official was told that his party needed this corrupt leader in the coming elections and therefore could not afford to offend him.

To help solve these problems, Barzani proposed elections for both a legislative council and supreme Kurdish leader: "There is crisis within the Kurdistan Front—a decisionmaking crisis. . . . In order for there to be a decisionmaking center and for this center to enjoy legitimacy, we decided that elections must be held . . . to determine which party, or parties, enjoy the masses' confidence."[9]

Talabani "hope[d] that the elections will result in the establishment of a legitimate, constitutional, and legal entity embodied in a council that will represent the Kurdish people and will be the political decisionmaking body in Iraqi Kurdistan."[10] Dr. Kamal Fuad, the official in charge of foreign relations in PUK, added that "the only solution to the Iraqi Kurdistan situation is through the parliamentary elections for the people of Kurdistan. The Kurdish parliament will form the civil administration and will act as the Kurdish northern government."[11]

Although Barzani and Talabani denied that there were serious differences between them, it was clear that the elections could offer the Kurds different futures.[12] Doubting the staying power of the West, Barzani favored some type of autonomy in agreement with Baghdad. The KDP leader also believed that anything more radical would not win the approval of Iraq's neighbors, who feared a nascent Kurdish state. On the other hand, Talabani favored self-determination within a democratic Iraq that would grant the Kurds more self-rule than the simple autonomy Barzani envisioned. Any talks with Baghdad would have to be carried out through the United Nations. To appease Iraq's neighbors, both men stressed that they were not seeking independence.

Initially announced in January 1992 and scheduled for April 3, the elections were first postponed until April 30 and then May 17 for technical reasons relating to the type of election system to be used and the location of polling centers. Finally they were delayed for another forty-eight hours because of a controversy over indelible ink to be used as an assurance against double voting.

Mechanics

Although he preferred a constituency system so that independent candidates could be elected, Barzani finally agreed to one of proportional representation because of the wishes of the other members in the Kurdish Front. It was then decided that the legislature would have a total of 105 members, one for every 30,000 people.[13] To win seats in this body, it would be necessary to win at least 7 percent of the vote, a provision that proved to shut out all but the KDP and PUK. At the same time as this legislature would be chosen, a supreme executive leader who had received at least 51 percent of the vote also would be picked.

The electorate consisted of some 1.1 million men and women over the age of eighteen eligible to vote. The legislative candidates had to be citizens and residents of Kurdistan, at least thirty years old, sane, literate, and not convicted of any unethical or corrupt activities, murder, theft, or crimes committed or planned by Baghdad. Barzani and Talabani were the two leading candidates for the supreme leadership position, but two others also contended.

Apparently only seven of the eight reputed members of the Kurdish Front participated in the elections; the SPKI of Rasul Mamand and Mahmud Uthman and the Kurdish Socialist Party (PASOK) supposedly had united one month earlier.[14] The names of the Front's parties were listed in alphabetical order and according to a special color: (1) yellow for the KDP, (2) blue for the SPKI and PASOK, (3) black and blue for the KPDP, (4) white with a red star for the Kurdistan Toilers Party, (5) red for the ICP-Kurdish Section, (6) indigo for the Assyrian Democratic Movement, and (7) green for the PUK. Various Islamic parties also seem to have participated.

On the other hand, the Iraqi National Turkoman Party (IMTP), which was not a member of the Kurdish Front, decided not to participate in the elections. To do so "would mean a de facto recognition of Kurdistan and acknowledgment that the Turkomans were part of it" and possibly would provoke "Iraqi harassment" of the Turkomans "since they [the Turkomans] were living in a concentrated way in the province of Karkuk which was under Iraqi control."[15] Muzaffer Aslan, the leader of the IMTP, also declared his party would "not take part in an election which threatens Iraq's territorial integrity."[16] Since the IMTP was now head-quartered in Ankara, Turkey, it presumably reflected Turkish fears on this score.

In addition, the PKK—the Kurdish Workers Party in Turkey, which was waging a guerrilla war against Turkey increasingly from camps in northern Iraq—did not participate in the elections. Apparently, the Kurdish Front decided to exclude it because "those who do not join the battle fronts cannot participate in the elections."[17] The desire not to antagonize further its new Turkish ally undoubtedly also played a role in the Front's actions here.

On the eve of the elections, the leaders of the eight members of the Kurdish Front signed in Arbil a "Sacred, Historic Kurdish Covenant" that pledged that nothing would "disturb or impede them [the elections] or distort their soundness, honesty, and legitimacy."[18] They also declared their "respect for the outcome of the elections and . . . full and uncondi-tional commitment to whatever its results will be, [and] to the decisions of the Kurdistan National Council and the laws it will enact."

Results

Despite these professions of goodwill, there were a number of charges of voting fraud. The smaller parties, which failed to win any seats in the new parliament because of the 7 percent requirement, raised protests of widespread double voting and usage of forged identifications. The ink manufactured locally to mark voters in the absence of official registers, for example, turned out to be easily wiped off by small amounts of acid from automobile batteries. At one polling station hundreds of eager vot-ers were locked out. Mahmud Uthman declared: "There was so much cheating that if you want to investigate, you have to investigate every-where."[19]

On the other hand, Michael Meadowcroft of the London-based Elec-toral Reform Society pronounced the results "free and fair." He said that his group of forty-six observers had watched 141 of the 176 polling sta-tions and had discovered "no evidence" of "substantial fraud that would have significantly affected the results."[20] Although the announcement of the results was delayed in an attempt to solve any remaining problems, the smaller parties eventually accepted what had occurred.

In the parliamentary voting, the KDP won 50.22 percent and the PUK 49.78 percent of the vote.[21] These figures apparently represented the distribution after the votes of those parties that had not received at least 7 percent of the vote were eliminated. Although they were nevertheless offered seats, the smaller parties turned the proposal down. After much negotiation, the Kurdish Front decided that the KDP and the PUK would each be given fifty seats in the National Council. The remaining five would be given to the Christian minority with four of these going to the Assyrian Democratic Movement.[22]

As part of the agreement, it also was decided the chairman of the National Council would be from the KDP, while his deputy would be from the PUK. Conversely, the chairman of the Executive Council would be from the PUK and his deputy from the KDP.[23] According to one report, new elections were to be held in October, but this did not occur.

The balloting for a supreme leader gave Barzani 466,819 votes and Talabani 441,057, with two other candidates receiving less than 40,000.[24] Barzani decisively beat Talabani in the Dohuk area, but only edged him out around Arbil. In the Sulaymaniya area, on the other hand, Talabani won a clear victory. Since Barzani did not win a majority, a second round of voting was necessary to choose the leader, but for practical reasons this also would not be possible in the near future. The result was a disappointment to Barzani, who had originally insisted on such an election, while Talabani had demurred.

Nevertheless, once the compromise had been reached, Barzani and Talabani announced that "the elections were a victory for everyone."[25] In an later interview, however, Talabani owned that "everyone ended up dissatisfied with the results."[26] His PUK had hoped to win 55 to 60 percent of the votes, the KDP had been counting on 70 percent, and the smaller parties also had hoped to do better.

The PUK leader argued, however, that he "personally believe[d] that the elections proved that the Kurdish people are worthy of freedom and capable of engaging in democracy and the electoral process, despite the lack of experience." The elections also showed that "this people can exercise government in their region and that they deserve to enjoy the right to self- determination within a unified democratic Iraq." Although there had been "dissent and objections," the result was one "which all Kurdish parties accepted, albeit reluctantly, in order to safeguard the unity of Kurdish ranks and to portray the Kurds as civilized people before the world."

Barzani declared that "these elections were positive and a major step for us."[27] He admitted that "due to the fact that this was our first election, we had some technical and other problems," but claimed that "we will overcome these shortcomings in future elections."

Although Baghdad had denounced the elections as "high treason, . . . plotting against Iraq, [and] its territorial integrity,"[28] Barzani still maintained that "our goal is not to set up an independent state."[29] Talabani shared this sentiment by declaring at the same time: "We do not want to break away from Iraq; we want a democratic Iraq."[30]

Shortly after he had returned from his trip to Turkey and Europe in February and March 1992, Barzani had explained his reasoning here: "The situation in the world today is such that it will not permit any changes in regional borders. Nor will it stand for any partitioning."[31] Therefore, argued the leader of the KDP, the Iraqi Kurds should "not swim against the international tide. We should act with wisdom . . . [and] bear in mind that there is a wide gap between our wishes and our rights on the one hand, and what we can achieve on the other."

FLEDGLING GOVERNMENT

Despite Talabani's and Barzani's words to the contrary, it was clear that the Kurds preferred an independent state and would declare one when they deemed the time propitious. In announcing their new unified party shortly after the May elections, for example, the SPKI, PASOK (now referred to as the Kurdistan Democratic Independence Party), and KPDP proclaimed "our Kurdish nation's right to self-determination, including the right to establish its independent state as a final objective."[32]

Visiting northern Iraq just after the Kurdish elections in May, a Turkish reporter noted how "the moment you step into Iraq from the Harbor border, the slogan 'Welcome to Kurdistan' [preceding three words in English] greets you."[33] When the same reporter finally arrived at the PUK headquarters in Shaqlawa, he was met by a similar sign: "Welcome to liberated Kurdistan." During his visit to the same sites a few months earlier, however, no such slogans had existed.

Asked whether Iraqi Kurdistan were moving to become an independent state, Dr. Kamal Fuad, a member of the PUK leadership, replied "Why not?" He cautioned, however, that the Kurds "have no such objective for the time being. We are currently merely filling in an administrative vacuum."

Before leaving, the same Turkish reporter was shown a map of the "two-thirds of Kurdistan" under the control of the Kurdish Front. It "was prepared by PUK's al-Sulaymaniyah Deputy (Umer Seyid Eli Husen) at considerable effort." Zakho, Dohuk, Arbil, and Sulaymaniya were included, while Mosul and Kirkuk were left out.

A report in late April 1992 indicated that the Kurds had started to export oil by truck to Turkey.[34] They had established a company called "Kurdoil" and were seeking U.N. permission for their activities. Some 20,000 to 25,000 barrels of oil a day were being hauled across the border and traded for foodstuffs and refined oil. Much greater amounts were projected. Despite its divisions, the Kurdish Front "somehow [had] come up with a modus vivendi to monitor Kurdoil operations to ensure that the oil exports will benefit all Kurds rather than areas which are loyal to any single group," said one source.[35]

A statement by the U.S. State Department further illustrated the Kurdish success regarding finances: "The Kurdish Front has raised enough to pay some salaries and maintain some semblance of a social services network."[36] By the end of May, cross-border trade between Turkey and the Iraqi Kurds reportedly "constituted a major break-through."[37] Turkish truck drivers were "required to pay large amounts of cash to [Kurdish] customs officials," while the Kurds received "Turkish food supplies at cheap rates."

In one of its first meetings the new Kurdish National Council, or parliament, discussed financial and economic affairs as well as the reopening of plants in the area. During the session, 5 million dinars were allocated for the salaries of employees and teachers. Three million of these dinars had been collected from the Kurdish Front's customs post in Dohuk; 2 million had come from the posts in Rawanduz and Raniya.[38]

These economic decisions followed the council's first meeting, which was held in Arbil on June 4, 1992. In the presence of Barzani and Talabani, the members had taken an oath regarding "the safeguarding of the people and the land of Kurdistan."[39] Jawhar Namiq Salim was elected as the council's speaker, and Muhammad Tawfiq Rahim, his deputy.

On July 4, the process of creating a government for the de facto Kurdish state was completed when Dr. Fuad Masum, the chairman of the council of ministers [rais majlis al-wuzara], announced the names of the ministers and their ministries. These included: Amin Mawlud, industry and electricity; Shirku Bakus, culture and information; Muhammad Tawfiq Rahim, humanitarian aid and cooperation; Dr. Salah-al-Din Hadid, finance and economy; Qadir Aziz Muhammad Amin, agriculture and irrigation; Mrs. Kathya Sulayman, municipalities and tourism; Kamal

Shakir, health and social affairs; Major General Kamal Mufti, military affairs—peshmergas; Marun al-Buriskani, reconstruction and development; Muhammad Mulla Abd-al-Qadir, Awqaf [religious endowments]; Dr. Nasih Ghafur, education; Yunadin Yusuf Kaffa, works and housing; Dr. Rusha Ways, interior (acting) and deputy prime minister; and Dr. Idris Hadi, transport and communications.[40] The justice ministry remained vacant until further notice.

This government included members only from the KDP, PUK, and one Christian. There was no one from the newly combined three parties (SPKI, KPDP, and PASOK, a group that began calling itself the "Unity Party of Kurdistan") because they had unsuccessfully demanded one of the three main ministries—interior, peshmergas, or humanitarian aid and cooperation—as well as one governor and several district officers and subdistrict directors. Nevertheless, the government felt that "the Kurdish people will support the cabinet as long as it is effective" because "the Kurdish Cabinet is our supreme policy-making and executive body."[41] In near exultation, the new government declared: "The salvation of part of Kurdistan is a great national event that deserves to be celebrated for generations to come."

From June 16 to 19, 1992, the second Iraqi opposition conference was held in Vienna.[42] Some 200 delegates representing more than forty different opposition groups attended, including the Kurds. Important groups such as the Supreme Assembly of the Islamic Revolution in Iraq (SAIRI) and the Shiite Dawa Party, however, did not.

The Kurds upset many of the Arab opposition groups by demanding that the conference recognize their right to self-determination and that Iraq's unity was voluntary in return for Kurdish participation among the opposition. Jawad al-Maliki, the chairman of the first opposition conference in Beirut and, as a member of the Dawa Party leadership, not present at the conference, rejected this Kurdish demand "as a step toward secession."[43] Many of those present obviously agreed.

When the Kurdish Front suggested that the area it controlled in northern Iraq be used as a temporary headquarters for the opposition provisional government, some non-Kurdish, Iraqi opposition figures denounced its "arrogance" for tying the proposal to "constitutional guarantees saying that force will not be used against the Kurds under any circumstances."[44] Talabani, who was chosen to head the conference's most important committee—the political one—also asked the conference to support the Kurdish Front's demand that it receive some of the frozen Iraqi funds. It was increasingly clear that the Kurds were developing a de facto government and state in the area of northern Iraq under their control.

♦   ♦   ♦

11

The Turkish Factor

Since its birth in the early 1920s, the Turkish Republic has perceived Kurdish national awareness as a mortal threat to its own territorial integrity. This position was set by the republic's founder, Mustafa Kemal Ataturk. Referring to the Kurdish uprisings in eastern Turkey during the 1920s, Ismet Inonu, Ataturk's famous lieutenant and successor, declared: "Only the Turkish nation is entitled to claim ethnic and national rights in this country. No other element has any such right."[1]

The modern Republic of Turkey itself was established only after a long and terrible struggle against the invading Greeks in the west, a lesser but still serious one against the Armenians in the east, and the diplomatic victory at Lausanne under which the victorious allies of World War I recognized the new situation. Nurtured on the Kemalist ideology of republican Turkey's national unity and territorial integrity, which had sprung from the earlier trauma of the gradual disintegration of the Ottoman Empire, the authorities attempted to eliminate much that might suggest a separate Kurdish nation.

A broad battery of devices was employed to achieve this aim. In some cases what can only be termed pseudotheoretical justifications were offered to defend what was being done. Thus, both Turks and Kurds were taught that they were descended from the pure Turkish race. Isolated in the mountain fastnesses of eastern Anatolia, the Kurds had simply forgotten their mother tongue. The much-abused and criticized appellation "mountain Turks" when referring to the Turkish Kurds served as a code term for these actions.

The obvious purpose was to make the Turkish Kurds not only politically Turks (as legally they already were) but also culturally and socially Turks through assimilation. Even the Kurdish language was constitutionally "prohibited by law" for use "in the expression and dissemination of thought,"[2] a stipulation reinforced in 1983 by Law 2932. During the

1970s and 1980s, Dr. Ismail Besikci, a Turkish sociologist and possibly the cause célébre of the cases dealing with the suppression of the Turkish Kurds, spent more than a decade in prison for maintaining in his scholarly work that the Kurds constitute a separate, ethnic group.

The response many Turks made in 1991 to President Turgut Ozal's modest proposals to rescind Law 2931 illustrates how the term "Kurd" still remained a four-letter word for many of them. Suleyman Demirel, the former prime minister who was reelected to that post on October 20, 1991, declared, for example:

> Opening the Kurdish problem to discussion would lead to the disintegration of a country in which people from 26 different ethnic groups live. That is why I say that dealing with the Kurdish problem is playing with fire.... The moment we begin discussing the Kurdish problem, we create an atmosphere of estrangement among the citizens.... People from other ethnic groups will ask: What about us?... This move is an attempt at dividing the country.... This is the greatest harm you can inflict on Turkey. Whoever plans to undermine Turkey's unity and solidarity and takes steps in that direction is involved in irresponsibility, corruption, and treachery.[3]

Others expressed themselves less forthrightly. In response to the query whether the new Ozal proposal would permit the manufacture of audiocassettes and the printing of books in Kurdish, the minister of justice, Oltan Sungurlu, replied: "What language is that? I do not know of such a language."[4] Illustrating the foot-in-the-door fear that yielding language rights today would lead to demands for independence in the future, the chairman of the justice committee in the Turkish Parliament, Alpaslan Pehlivanli, expressed his concerns in the following manner:

> If the word "language" now in the bill stays in, we will have admitted that the Kurds are a nation.... If it passes this way, tomorrow there will be cafes where Kurdish folk songs are sung, theaters where Kurdish films are shown, and coffee houses where Kurdish is spoken. If this is not separatism, what is?[5]

OZAL'S INITIATIVE

Since Ozal studied and worked in the United States on two separate occasions in his career, he presumably has been exposed to Western concepts of individual rights and pluralism. Nevertheless, he long continued Turkey's traditional policy towards the Kurds. In September 1989, however, while still prime minister, he hinted at a reassessment in his cryptic response to a question about the existence of a Kurdish minority in Turkey: "If in the first years of the Republic, during the single-party period, the State committed mistakes on this matter, it is necessary to recognise these."[6]

In April 1990 Ozal gave further hints of a new Kurdish policy at the meeting of the Turkish Industrialists' and Businessmen's Association (TUSIAD). At this time he let it be known that the government was "engaged in a quest for a serious model for solving the Kurdish problem in a manner that goes beyond police measures."[7] At about the same time, Abdullah (Apo) Ocalan, the general secretary of the Partiya Karkaren Kurdistan (PKK) or Kurdish Workers Party told two Turkish reporters: "Let us declare a cease-fire and sit at the negotiating table. If Turkey abandons its oppressive policy in the region, then we will refrain from violence. . . . In fact, separating the region from Turkey immediately is out of the question. Our people need Turkey and we cannot separate, at least not for another 40 years."[8] Coming from the leader of the main Kurdish insurgency movement in Turkey, this statement deserved consideration.

In the summer of 1990, the main opposition party in Turkey (after the elections of October 20, 1991, the junior partner in the new coalition government headed by Suleyman Demirel) the Social Democratic Populist Party (SDPP), issued a comprehensive policy report on the Kurdish problem that went far beyond anything ever before offered by a mainstream Turkish party. Describing the ban on the use of the mother tongue as "primitive" and a "tool of assimilation," the document called for: "the abolition of all restrictions on the use of the mother tongue, the enshrinement of the right of citizens to speak, write and teach their own language and use it in daily life and in various cultural activities and the establishment by the state of research centres and institutes undertaking research into different cultures and languages."[9]

On the other hand, following Ozal's meeting with the leaders of the three parties in parliament, the government had issued on April 9, 1990, Decree 413, which granted the regional governor in the southeast, Hayri Kozakcioglu, extraordinary powers to censor the press, exile people who present a "danger to law and order," remove judges and public prosecutors, and suspend trade union rights. In addition, Kozakcioglu was even given authority to ban or confiscate publications outside of his jurisdiction in the southeast.[10]

The 1991 Gulf War acted as a catalyst to Ozal's thinking and the subsequent initiatives of the new prime minister, Suleyman Demirel. Suddenly world attention was turned to events on the Turkish border, and Turkey quickly became an important allied associate. What is more, Iraq's defeat would threaten Turkey, because the creation of a Kurdish state in northern Iraq could act like a magnet for Turkey's own restless Kurds. The Kurdish problems in Iraq and Turkey—so long segregated from each other—became partially fused by the various forces let loose by the war.

Although Ozal made it clear that Turkey would not tolerate a Kurdish state in northern Iraq, he was also farsighted enough to contemplate a more imaginative response than mere negativism. Analyzing his country's past position on the Kurds, the Turkish president declared: "A policy of repression was adopted with the aim of assimilating them. That was a mistake."[11] If Turkey could successfully move to settle its own Kurdish problem, then the Iraqi Kurds might begin to see Turkey as a protector instead of an enemy. To accomplish this, Ozal moved in at least three ways: He presented the language bill, met with representatives of the Iraqi Kurds, and granted an amnesty which also applied to many Turkish Kurds such as the former mayor of Diyarbakir, Mehdi Zana.

Language Bill

In repealing Law 2932, Ozal was legalizing the use of Kurdish only in a limited way: Kurdish could only be used in everyday conversation and folkloric music recordings. Using the language in official agencies, publishing, or teaching would still be a crime. Asked when Kurdish could be used in newspapers, audiocassettes, radio broadcast, and schools, Ozal replied: "In the future the use of the written language may also be allowed, but everything has its time."[12] Similarly Metin Gurdere, the assistant leader of the ruling Motherland Party (ANAP), said that further liberalization "would depend on developments that will take place in Turkey."[13]

Despite its patent limitations, Ozal's initiative caused a sensation both in Turkey and the West. Most Turkish politicians seemed cautiously to approve.[14] Even former president Kenan Evren, who had led the military takeover and had been the architect of the laws reinforcing the prohibition of the use of Kurdish and especially Law 2932, expressed his guarded support "as long as this does not enter the schools or appear on placards during demonstrations." Erdal Inonu, the leader of the SDPP, said that it was a positive step and that he was pleased that the government finally had accepted a policy that was originally his. Husamettin Cindoruk of Demirel's True Path Party (DYP) said the initiative was an "end of a constitutional embarrassment."

Opposition, however, existed. In the ruling ANAP party opinion seemed to be divided three ways: those who thought the bill was useless, as it created no real change in practice; the nationalist faction who believed that the bill could lead to further demands and were, therefore, opposed to it; and those who thought it was a cautious step forward. Among the first group were members of parliament from constituencies in the southeast with mainly Kurdish-speaking populations. These parliamentarians wanted to see Kurdish allowed at public gatherings, in films, the arts, newspapers, state offices, and education. One even suggested that Kurdish be declared the second official language of Turkey.

Nurettin Yilmaz, an outspoken ANAP member in parliament from Mardin and a strong supporter of Kurdish rights, not only called the Ozal proposal worthless but then went on to make several other declarations that served to bring out some of the latent discrimination existing on the party's right. Addressing the ANAP parliament members, Yilmaz told them: "You [Turks] are not from here [Anatolia]. You came from Central Asia. Aside from you, there are twenty million Kurds living on this land."

The repeated references to "you" and "we" angered the right-wing nationalist parliamentarians, provoking strong insults and abuse. Mustafa Tasar shouted at Yilmaz, "You're a separatist. . . . Get down from there!" When Yilmaz replied that he was a nationalist, Tasar answered, "Yes, you're a Kurdish nationalist." Yildaz, however, continued, telling the deputies that Kurdish should be taught in the schools and that 80 percent of those killed during the battle of Gallipoli during World War I were Kurds. When he finally stepped down, the room erupted in fury with such ANAP deputies as Ercument Konukman, Alpaslan Pehlivanli, Hasan Celal Guzel, and Gokhan Maras drumming their desktops in protest.

For the most part, the press also reacted with cautious approval to the Ozal initiative. Mehmet Ali Birand, possibly the most distinguished Turkish journalist, noted how this step would improve Turkey's image in Europe. Ertugrul Ozkok of Hurriyet found Ozal's move "the first positive consequence of the war." Oktay Eksi, from the same publication, stated that "we must thus acknowledge with satisfaction the ANAP's initiative, or rather, Turgut Ozal's, to abolish this shameful prohibition of a language." He warned, however, that "there is no reason to be so naive as to believe that this new attitude is motivated only by a concern for the respect of human rights."

On the other hand, Ugur Mumcu of Cumhuriyet pointed out that there were still various other laws concerning separatist propaganda that could be used against the Turkish Kurds and their supporters. He also recalled that the political parties law still prohibited parties from asserting that any minorities existed in the country. Mumcu explained Ozal's initiative in terms of the Gulf War and the possible creation of a Kurdish state in northern Iraq. Taha Akyol of Tercuman, and a former member of Alparslan Turkes' right-wing party, questioned whether "the Kurdish language will become an element of cultural enrichment for Turkey or whether, on the contrary, 'politicized' Kurdish will be transformed into a weapon in the radicalization of the processes of separation and division."

From the other side of the ideological spectrum, the famous sociologist Ismail Besikci responded that: "It is evident that plans for the Middle East which do not take into account the national existence and political demands of the Kurds will not be successful."[15] Former minister and parliamentary deputy Serafettin Elci, journalist and author Musa Anter, the owner of the weekly Yeni Ulke Serhat Bucak, and folk singer Rahmi Saltuk, all described the Ozal initiative as inadequate: "If the problem is speaking Kurdish, we were speaking it anyway. The important thing is cultural rights. It is Kurdish books, newspapers and magazines. It is Kurdish folklore being practiced freely, the ability to broadcast Kurdish radio and TV."[16]

Kendal Nezan, a Turkish Kurdish physicist who fled from Turkey in 1971 and has since become a major critic of the Turkish government's policies in his role as the director of the Kurdish Institute in Paris, reacted more positively:

> The bill is a positive step towards finding a peaceful, democratic, and civilized solution to the Kurdish problem in Turkey. . . . Mr. Ozal, a pragmatic and realistic statesman, is aware of how these outside balances and the policy of denying the existence of the Kurds in Turkey since 1924 have brought the country to an impasse. . . . Turgut Ozal is the first statesman . . . to accept and recognize the Kurdish presence in Turkey. . . . This return to the historical, social, and cultural facts after 67 years of ideological absurdity and blindness is no doubt positive.[17]

Abdullah (Apo) Ocalan, the general secretary of the PKK, concurred with Nezan's judgment: "To tell the truth, I did not expect him [Ozal] to display such courage. . . . In this context, he shamed us. . . . He has taken an important step."[18] At approximately the same time, Ocalan also announced that his group "might opt for a diplomatic-political solution" and was ready to hold "conditional" negotiations with Turkey.[19] He added that the PKK no longer sought independence, just "free political expression" for Turkey's Kurds.

DEMIREL RETURNS TO POWER

The elections of October 20, 1991, in Turkey resulted in the return to power of Suleyman Demirel and his True Path Party (DYP) in a coalition with Erdal Inonu's Social Democrats. By this time the PKK insurgency in Turkey was entering its eighth year. Some 3,300 people had been killed since August 1984. That very month 500 armed PKK struck a Turkish border post, killing 17 and wounding many more. Turkish soldiers were being kidnapped and held by the PKK. The PKK was issuing visas for foreigners to travel in southeastern Turkey. Foreign tourists were being kidnapped. And bloody riots in Diyarbakir followed the mysterious murder of the Kurdish leader, Vedat Aydin, in July 1991. Before the new government was even established, moreover, the Kurdish issue infringed upon the new parliament as its members were being sworn in.

In the fall of 1989, a number of parliamentary members of Inonu's party, who were of Kurdish ancestry, had been expelled for attending a conference on Kurdish issues in Paris. These former SDPP members were the seed of the Peoples Labor Party (HEP), which was formed in the spring of 1990 to be, in effect, the legal, political organization of the Kurdish movement in Turkey. The party's founding congress could not be held in time for it to qualify for the 1991 elections. Therefore, in order to get elected, twenty-two HEP members rejoined the SDPP and were elected to the new parliament in October 1991.

Hatip Dicle and Leyla Zana, two of these former HEP members, caused an uproar in Turkey by their actions while being sworn in.[20] The oath they took included the words: "I swear . . . before the great Turkish nation . . . [the] indivisible integrity of the country and nation." Dicle, who held a handkerchief with the Kurdish national colors, prefaced these words by declaring that he did so under duress. Zana, wearing Kurdish national colors on her headband, added in Kurdish at the end of her oath that "I take this oath for the brotherhood of the Turkish and Kurdish peoples."

Illustrative of the ingrained nationalist fear and opposition to anything Kurdish still held by many, a number of members began to beat their desktops in the traditional form of protest for Turkey's parliament, while several angrily approached the rostrum. Inonu himself denounced the two former HEP members and called for their resignation, while other members of parliament termed their behavior "antidemocratic, uncivilised and a great number of other things." Bulent Ecevit, the former prime minister and current leader of the small Democratic Left

Party, declared: "My heart is crying tears of blood." The following morn-
ing the majority of the newspapers in Turkey carried headlines such as
"Nationwide Anger," "An Ugly Show in Parliament," and "Two Terrorist
MP's."

On the other hand, President Ozal simply said that Dicle and Zana
had not helped the cause of the citizens in the southeast. Prime Minister
designate Suleyman Demirel cooled the fires by adding that there was
nothing to panic about. Demirel's declaration proved to be the initial
salvo of a remarkable opening to Turkey's citizens of Kurdish extraction.

The Kurdish Reality

As he formally assumed office in November, Demirel described the
Kurdish situation as "Turkey's top problem."[21] In an exclusive interview,
the new prime minister declared: "Turkey's borders, flag, and official
language cannot be debated, but ethnic groups' demand to retain their
own ethnic identity and culture should not be rejected. They are already
using their own language. They have their own history, language, and
folklore. If they wish to develop them, let them do so."[22]

His deputy prime minister, Erdal Inonu, added that one and a half
years earlier, his party had issued a detailed report on the situation that
recommended a number of major reforms. Now, finally in power, Inonu
declared: "The Kurdish citizens' cultural identity must be recognized in
full. That is, we must acknowledge the reality that some of our citizens
are not Turks but Kurds who belong to the Republic of Turkey."[23]

In a joint report, the new coalition government affirmed:

> The era of seeking rights by arms, violence, and terrorism has come to an end.
> The conditions of our time have created peaceful rules and institutions for the
> pursuit and preservation of rights. The CSCE [Conference on Security and
> Cooperation in Europe] and the Paris Condition have introduced global rules,
> rights, and freedoms for all countries and peoples. As a signatory to these
> agreements, Turkey must also comply with these rules. A state of law based on
> human rights and basic freedoms will definitely be established across our
> entire country.... Diversity does not weaken a democratic and unitary state....
> Everyone's right to research, to preserve and to develop his mother tongue,
> culture, history, folklore, and religious beliefs is part of his basic human rights
> and freedoms. These rights will be guaranteed within the framework of laws.[24]

In proclaiming these major concessions to Kurdish rights, the new
Demirel government made it clear that it expected terrorism to end and
loyalty to the Turkish government to be renewed: "Attacks against the

existence and democratic authority of the state through violence and terrorism is incompatible with human rights and basic freedoms and cannot be acceptable."[25]

To announce their intentions and study the situation firsthand, on December 7 and 8 Demirel and Inonu journeyed to five southeastern provinces: Diyarbakir, Siirt, Batman, Sirnak, and Mardin. With them were the chief of the general staff Dogan Gures, state ministers Akin Gonen and Mehmet Kahraman, Defense Minister Nevzat Ayaz, Interior Minister Ismet Sezgin, and Gendarmerie Commander Esref Bitlis. The high-level nature of this delegation emphasized the importance the new government attached to the Kurdish problem.

Addressing tens of thousands of cheering Turkish Kurdish citizens in Diyarbakir, Demirel declared that "Turkey has recognized the Kurdish reality."[26] Before the building where Demirel and Inonu addressed the people of Sirnak, "Turkish flags mingled with the green, yellow and red rags symbolizing the Kurdish flag, held by Kurdish women cheering in support of the coalition."[27] By the end of the trip, the heretofore feared and distant chief of the general staff, General Dogan Gures, could not resist calling out in the once-forbidden Kurdish language to a local child. "Demirel and Inonu are now our fathers. We trust them and we will support their policies," exclaimed one former HEP partisan from the Mardin township of Midyat.

The PKK had asked its supporters not to try to disrupt the government's procession. Ocalan even declared that "Demirel is truly a respected politician."[28] The hardened PKK leader queried, however, whether the new Turkish prime minister could carry out his stated intentions:

> We are doubtful there will be a change. For one, will Demirel be able to control the chief of [the] general staff? Will he be able to place the special warfare and counter-guerrilla [activities] under his control? ... They are the true forces of power. ... Will the Demirel-Inonu government be able to overthrow these forces from power? ... As you know, Demirel was toppled from power twice [1971 and 1980] and he was not in control.[29]

RENEWED VIOLENCE

The renewed violence that occurred during the 1992 *Nawroz* holiday in March 1992 illustrated that the fighting would not only continue but would escalate. In stark contrast to the official, government view "that terrorists equipped with heavy arms launched an armed action against the state,"[30] the SDPP—the junior member of the coalition government—reported that "excessive use of force by security troops and provocation may have been behind the confrontation which claimed more than 70 lives in a matter of ten days."[31] In Sarnak, where officials claimed that a PKK attack had taken place, the SDPP report quoted reliable local sources that security forces had simply opened fire on the townspeople, not the terrorists. The fact that the security forces suffered no casualties gave credence to this report. Similarly, a Helsinki Watch report concluded that "the Turkish military and police forces . . . were directly responsible for almost every casualty that took place during Nevroz."[32]

What is more, a series of mysterious killings of civilian Kurdish leaders by apparent right-wing, government hit squads (the "Hizballah-contras") that had begun in the summer of 1991 continued. One report claimed that as many as 225 assassinations had occurred.[33] Another pointed out that, while more than 4,000 "separatist suspects" had been detained since January 1992, not a single one of the slayings of Kurdish leaders or sympathizers had resulted in an arrest: "Many of the individual killings still go unexplained amid local claims that certain officials prefer not to pursue such cases."[34]

Ocalan declared that "the effort by the Erdal Inonu-Suleyman Demirel coalition to implement moderate measures has not achieved anything."[35] Government statements that it would recognize the Kurdish reality were "insufficient"[36] and "words alone."[37] "Nevruz has marked the beginning of a hot summer. . . . Violence may increase in 1992."[38] "The Turkish Government has to be open to the idea of a federation. If 10 million Kurds live in Turkey, they must have their own political will, national assembly, government, and culture."[39] Trying possibly to divide Ozal and Demirel even more than had already occurred, Ocalan also declared that the Turkish president "understands us better than anyone else. . . . If anyone is going to find a way to solve our problem, Ozal will."[40] For Demirel, however, he had only scathing words: "He has tried to destroy us. . . . From now on, we will adopt an open stand against Demirel."

In analyzing the failure of Demirel's initiative, what Donald L. Horowitz, a well-known authority on ethnic conflict, has termed "the timeliness of the arrangements"[41] comes to mind. Had these reforms been instituted earlier, they might have worked better. As Horowitz also pointed, however: "there will generally not be the requisite determination to enact appropriate measures until ethnic conflict has already advanced to a dangerous level; but by that time the measures that are adopted are more likely to be deflected or ineffective."[42] Thus, reforms that might have worked earlier will not work now.

THE DEVELOPING RELATIONSHIP BETWEEN
TURKEY AND THE IRAQI KURDS

As mentioned, because of the 1991 Gulf War, Turkey and the Iraqi Kurds suddenly became very important for each other. President Ozal even declared that "it must be made clear that those in the Iraqi Kurdish area are relatives of Turkish citizens. So the borders are to some extent artificial, dividing people into two sections."[43] For the leader of a state that until recently had not even recognized that Kurds lived in Turkey, this statement illustrated how greatly the thinking on the Kurdish issue was changing.

There were a variety of reasons why Turkey now sought to protect and, in effect, promote the Iraqi Kurds. For one thing, if the Iraqi Kurds were dependent on Turkish goodwill, Turkey might be able to influence them from establishing their own state, which could conceivably have a dangerous demonstration effect on the Turkish Kurds. Additionally, an unfriendly Iraqi Kurdish state might begin aiding the PKK or even make territorial claims on Turkey's Kurdish region. On the other hand, by supporting the Iraqi Kurds Turkey might influence them to be pro-Turkish and thus help to solve its own Kurdish problem more readily. Third, if Saddam were to crush the Kurds again, Turkey might have to face hordes of destabilizing Kurdish refugees once more. Finally, being looked upon as the protector of the Iraqi Kurds would win Turkey respect and support in the West, where Turkey sought eventual membership in the European Economic Community.

Accordingly, Prime Minister Demirel favored the extension of Operation Poised Hammer for another four months after it was scheduled to expire on June 28, 1992. Turkish approval was necessary because this multilateral Western force to protect the Iraqi Kurds from Saddam was stationed on Turkish territory. "This . . . is a force which says, 'I am here' in order to prevent the people who have been subjected to Saddam Hossein's tyranny in the past from falling into new difficulties,"[44] explained Demirel. "We cannot watch another Halabja."

Others explained the Turkish position in a more realistic manner as a "no-win situation,"[45] since by allowing Operation Poised Hammer to continue, Turkey in effect was reinforcing de facto Kurdish statehood. To abandon the force, however, would simply lead it to regroup elsewhere and strip Ankara of any influence whatsoever over the course of events. At best, some argued, "Turkey appears to have been selling support for the multilateral force against silence on its own Kurdish question."[46] Accordingly, the Turkish parliament voted in favor of renewing

Operation Poised Hammer, although it added the proviso that the territorial integrity of Iraq must be respected. This meant, of course, that Turkey opposed the creation of a Kurdish state. Turkey also opposed the elections held by the Iraqi Kurds in May 1992, fearing that they would accelerate the process of developing a Kurdish state.

For their part, the Iraqi Kurds felt dependent on Turkey. Hoshyar Zevari, a spokesman for the KDP, explained: "Turkey is our lifeline to the West and the whole world in our fight against Saddam Husayn. We are able to secure allied air protection and international aid through Turkey's cooperation. If Poised Hammer is withdrawn, Saddam's units will again reign in this region and we will lose everything."[47]

When he went to Turkey in late 1991, Talabani concluded that "Turkey must be considered a country friendly to the Kurds."[48] By the time he met with Demirel in June 1992, the Turkish prime minister was referring to the PUK leader as "my dear brother Talabani,"[49] while the Iraqi Kurdish leader declared that "the people in northern Iraq will never forget the help of the Turkish Government and people in their difficult days."

In furtherance of this emerging Turkish-Iraqi Kurdish alliance, Barzani denounced "as savagery the incidents caused by the terrorist PKK . . . organization on the occasion of the Nevruz festival."[50] After briefing his Turkish guests on his contacts in Europe, the KDP leader then "requested technical aid from Turkey, especially in the field of agriculture and livestock,"[51] an overture Turkey was predisposed to grant. Rasul Mamand also journeyed to Ankara in April to head a joint delegation of his SPKI and the Kurdistan Democratic Independence Party (PASOK) in talks with Turkish Minister of State Mehmet Kahraman on violations of human rights and the Turkish position on humanitarian aid and Kurdistan.

By the end of 1991, the Iraqi Kurds had two representatives or de facto ambassadors in place in Ankara: Mohsin Dizai for the KDP and Serchil Kazzaz for the PUK. They were joined in 1992 by a representative of the SPKI, Dr. Hayrullah Ahmet Salih. No Turkish official, however, was formally named to reciprocate.

The only serious problem that seemed to cloud the emerging alliance was the Turkish bombing of reputed PKK camps in northern Iraq, which resulted in Iraqi Kurdish deaths. So strongly did Barzani feel about this issue that in October 1991 he almost broke off the Turkish connection. The need for Turkish support far outweighed this problem, however, so the emerging alliance continue to blossom. Nevertheless, lingering difficulty over the bombing remained. Indeed, after more Turkish attacks early in June 1992, a spokesman for the KDP declared: "They [the Turks] are breaking their commitment not to attack civilian villages."[52]

Bitterly he added: "It is very clear the Turkish military is not interested in the political dialogue we are having with their civilian government."[53] Similarly, Barzani himself expressed discouragement over the Turkish opposition to the Iraqi Kurdish elections in May when he declared: "I'm dismayed by the Turkish Foreign Ministry statement because we have explained to top Turkish officials . . . and made it perfectly clear that these elections are not aimed at setting up an independent state."[54]

PKK–Iraqi Kurdish Relationship

At first glance it might be expected that, since they were all Kurds, the PKK and the various Iraqi Kurdish groups would be natural allies. A brief knowledge of the bitter divisions in Kurdish society, of course, would quickly eradicate that notion. In addition, of course, the divide-and-rule strategies of the states containing Kurdish populations have reinforced these Kurdish divisions.

Interestingly enough, at one time or another the PKK has been allied with both the KDP and the PUK. In July 1983, for example, the PKK and the KDP signed an accord termed "Principles of Solidarity" under which they each agreed upon a unified commitment against "every kind of imperialism, with American imperialism at the top of the list, and the struggle against the plans and plots of imperialism in the region."[55] The two parties also committed themselves to "cooperating with other revolutionary forces in the region and the creation of new alliances." Another provision of their protocol emphasized that the struggle "should depend on the force of the Kurdish people." Article 10 of the agreement stated that neither party should interfere in the internal affairs of the other or commit actions that could damage the other. The eleventh and final article declared that if one of them made a mistake in implementing their alliance and ignored a warning from the other, then the alliance could be terminated.

At first the accord worked well for both parties. PKK militants being trained in Syrian and Lebanese camps were slowly moved to northern Iraq, where new camps were established. PKK leaders apparently travelled mostly through Tehran and then to northern Iraq, while the "foot soldiers" moved from Syria, as armed groups over the Turkish border near Silopi and Cizre. From there they travelled on foot over the Silopi-Sarnak-Uludere path into northern Iraq.

Soon the Lolan camp, located in the triangle of land where Turkey, Iran, and Iraq meet, became the PKK's largest base in its new found sanctuary. This camp also contained the PKK press and publications center, as well as the KDP's headquarters and clandestine radio stations. It was at this time in 1984 that Barzani and Ocalan met each other in Damascus for the first and apparently only time.[56]

Relations between the KDP and the PKK began to cool in 1985 because of the PKK's violence against women and children and even members of the KDP itself. In May 1987 the KDP issued a warning to the PKK, as required under their 1983 agreement. In this warning the KDP declared that "it is clear they [the PKK] have adopted an aggressive attitude towards the leadership of our party, towards its policies and the friends of our party."[57] Barzani's KDP denounced what it termed "terrorist operations within the country and abroad and their actions to liquidate human beings. . . . The mentality behind such action is against humanity and democracy and is not in line with the national liberation of Kurdistan." Turkish pressures also played a role in ending the PKK-KDP alliance, which was severed completely by the end of 1987.

On May 1, 1989, Talabani and Ocalan apparently met and signed a "Protocol of Understanding" in Damascus[58] that called for strengthening Kurdish unity and for cooperation and joint action by Kurdish groups. Indeed, the PUK leader even threatened to give overt support to Ocalan if Turkey again entered northern Iraq.[59] Within a year, however, Ocalan declared the protocol "null and void."[60]

Once the 1991 Gulf War began to bring the Turks and Iraqi Kurds together, the Iraqi Kurdish Front declared on October 7 its intention to "combat the PKK."[61] Although the Turkish bombing of PKK camps in northern Iraq momentarily caused Barzani to consider rescinding this decision, the logic of the Turkish alliance prevailed.

Talabani apparently made one last attempt to bring Ocalan around by arguing that the "PKK must respond positively to Ozal's statement [on Kurdish rights] by halting its armed activities and by looking for a dialogue with the Turkish Government."[62] Late in November the PUK leader reported that the PKK had agreed to a four-month cease-fire so long as Turkey did not initiate any further hostilities: "Abdullah Ocalan will not resort to armed activities until Nowruz [March 21]."[63] The reputed guarantee came after a month of direct contacts between the PKK and the Iraqi Kurds who were acting for the Turks. One of the PKK negotiators was even quoted as saying: "The PKK no longer pursues a claim of independence and does not want any further bloodshed."[64] Ocalan went on to declare: "They say we are separatists and want to separate. This is nonsense! We have 900 years of togetherness with Turkey."[65] At the same time, however, the European Committee of the PKK based in Germany denied that the organization had agreed to a cease-fire and declared that attacks in the southeast of Turkey would continue.[66]

In the middle of December 1991, Ocalan reportedly crossed into northern Iraq to meet Talabani at his headquarters. Their meeting took place amid reports that Talabani's peshmergas had arrested seven members of the PKK Central Committee. Although no statement was issued by the two Kurdish leaders, presumably they failed to come to an agreement. Shortly afterward Ocalan sarcastically declared that Talabani had written him from Ankara to "lay down your arms unilaterally, accept a cease-fire, come to Ankara and sit at the table with obscure people, and be thankful and grateful for whatever you are given."[67]

Defiant, Ocalan declared: "I am allergic to such letters," adding that "if they try to make us collaborate, we will react with more fervor than they could muster to defend that policy." Talabani was then told "to forget about the 'new world order,' 'U.S. support,' and 'freedom to the Kurds,' slogans," and instead "join the militarization and resistance effort . . . [and] not act as a minor broker in dealing with the people."

For Barzani, Ocalan had even unkinder remarks: "Barzani does the same job in a more pompous manner."[68] The KDP leader "had made very bad business dealings in Kurdish blood. His is the policy of a broker."

In February 1992 the Iraqi Kurdish Front issued a warning to the PKK that "if it failed to cease activities against Turkey, it would be purged from the region."[69] Talabani declared that "his party does not approve of activities directed against Turkey by the terrorist organization active in southeastern Anatolia,"[70] while Barzani maintained that "the behavior of the . . . [PKK] has led to the ruin of the reputation of Kurds everywhere."[71]

Ocalan called Barzani a "collaborator, . . . reactionary, feudal person and a primitive nationalist."[72] He accused both Barzani and Talabani "of trying to stab the PKK in the back by cooperating with Turkey and noted that the two leaders have signed their own death warrants."[73] The PKK leader added that "the first thing we must do is remove these leeches. . . . They espouse the views of the fascist Turks. These two leaders are now our enemies."

Ocalan went on to argue that his party now had "a sister organization"[74] in Iraq, the Kurdish Liberation Party, which would be able to challenge Barzani and Talabani on their own grounds and "isolate" them. The PKK had "drawn up" this new Iraqi Kurdish party's "ideological and political aims." While "the PKK is waging a struggle for the liberation of the Kurds in Turkey," this new party "is waging a struggle for the liberation of the Kurds in Iraq."

In the summer of 1992 these intra-Kurdish diatribes broke out into open hostilities. The PKK threatened to cut the Iraqi Kurds' economic lifeline by successfully placing an embargo on trade between Turkey and northern Iraq. This trade interdiction proved so effective that it also called into question the very authority of the Turkish state. During the autumn the Iraqi Kurds launched major assaults against the PKK in an attempt to drive it from Khwakork, its base in the triangle where northern Iraq meets Turkey and Iran.

PKK and Saddam

The PKK position in northern Iraq became of more than academic interest when Turkish pressure finally forced Syria to evict the party from its longtime stronghold in the Bekaa Valley in late April 1992. With the apparent covert approval of Baghdad and taking advantage of the anarchy there, Ocalan's party reputedly relocated itself in northern Iraq. If it did so, cooperation between Saddam and the PKK was nothing new.

Despite its overt cooperation with Turkey during the Iran- Iraq War (1980-1988), some Turkish officials charged that at the same time Iraq secretly had supplied weapons to the PKK in return for information about the KDP. One Turkish officer explained: "The Iraqi regime has an interest in the border region where they cannot enter because of Barzani forces."[75] He added that "they [the Iraqis] give weapons and ammunition to the PKK in order to receive information on activities of Iraqi Kurds. The PKK while on one hand receives support from those [Iraqi] Kurds on the other sells them out for its own survival."

Another report seconded this claim: "Baghdad is now reported supplying the PKK with guns and ammunition in exchange for information. The feeling is the PKK is telling Iraqi troops where Barzani's camps are."[76] If these reports of Iraqi duplicity are valid, they help explain why the Iraqi KDP broke its alliance with the PKK at the end of 1987.

After Saddam's defeat in the 1991 Gulf War, Turkish officials charged that "Ocalan and Saddam Husayn met in al-Mawsil some time ago and decided to cooperate."[77] "The Iraqi government is arming and supplying the Kurdish separatist movement . . . in retaliation for Turkey's close cooperation with allied forces during the Gulf War."[78] Talabani too agreed that the PKK "is cooperating with Saddam Husayn's administration,"[79] while Rasul Mamand said that "in the talks in Baghdad, they told us they were helping the Kurds in Turkey. This could be financial, or through providing arms."[80]

In June 1992 a Turkish source claimed that Saddam "has received Abdullah Ocalan . . . with open arms after the latter was evicted from al-Biqa' by Syria."[81] A PKK camp had been established thirty kilometers south of Mosul in territory near the Tigris River controlled by Iraqi forces. All the arms and training equipment from the former PKK camp in Syria had been transferred to their new one in Iraq.

Talabani identified Mosul and Baghdad as two cities where PKK militants had been seen.[82] "I don't know where PKK leader Abdullah Ocalan is but he may be in Baghdad," said the PUK leader. To mollify the Turks, Talabani also declared: "We told them [the Turks] that the new [Kurdish] administration would try first to secure the area and control the borders," and then explained that "when it is able to control the border, the new administration will not permit such activities against Turkey."[83] Cleverly, the PUK leader also added that "controlling PKK activities out of northern Iraq also depended on the re-population of the border areas which was somewhat hindered by continuous Turkish air raids on alleged PKK targets in the area."

Early in July the two representatives of the Kurdish Front in Ankara stated that Saddam had secretly met with Ocalan in Baghdad the previous week.[84] However, Saddam had denied earlier in February that he was covertly supporting the PKK: "Definitely not. We do not support the PKK."[85] Seeking to play their own Kurdish card, Iraqi newspapers pointed out the "double standard" Turkey employed in claiming to protect the Iraqi Kurds while at the same time crushing the Turkish Kurds.[86]

As of July, therefore, the Iraqi Kurds were in an open but unofficial alliance with Turkey, while the PKK was apparently enjoying covert support from Iraq. Once again the Kurds were bitterly divided, as foreign governments sought to play them off against each other. This time, however, the Iraqi Kurds were in, what was for them at least, a uniquely stronger position. Saddam's folly in calling forth the allied attack against his country and the resulting allied and Turkish protection for the Kurds in northern Iraq helped to create a de facto Iraqi Kurdish government and state.

♦ ♦ ♦

12

Prospects

lthough it is not possible to read people's minds, it is difficult to believe that either side in the negotiations that followed the Kurdish uprising in March 1991 was doing more than buying time before the next round of fighting began. After all, that is what happened to previous negotiations in 1958 to 1961, during the 1960s, in 1970 to 1974, and in 1983 to 1984.

Saddam's objectives in starting the talks would seem to have been to neutralize the Kurdish resistance movement, play for time following his shattering defeat in the Gulf War, and divide the Iraqi opposition. To some extent, he initially accomplished all three of these goals.

The Kurds appeared to be waiting to see if Saddam could remain in power. Many seemed willing to seize control of various cities and towns in northern Iraq bit by bit, hoping that the threat of a renewed allied intervention would deter Baghdad from stopping them. All the posturing led observers to feel that history was repeating itself.

How long the current Iraqi leadership—with whom the Kurds were supposedly trying to obtain an agreement—could even last was questionable after the disaster of the Gulf War and the social problems caused by the continuing international sanctions against Iraq. If Saddam did fall—as eventually seemed likely—what good would any agreement be that he helped to author?

And what of those Kurdish leaders who led their people into another such disastrous rebellion? Did Talabani and Barzani learn nothing about the futility of depending on foreign promises, overt or implied? Even more, if the negotiations had turned out to have been a sham that had once again betrayed the Kurds, or if the Baathists successfully had broken the impasse and subdued them, what could have been said for the acuity of the Kurdish leadership?

Based on all this, it might be concluded that there may well be a day of reckoning for all these leaders associated with the events of 1991. Indeed, the Partiya Azadiya Kurdistan (PAK), or Kurdistan Liberation Party, was reported at the end of 1991 as constituting a new political entity "growing stronger constantly, especially in Diana [northern Iraq]" in reaction to the traditional Kurdish leadership.[1] This new organization had begun to wage "ideological war" against the Kurdish Front by accusing it of being "collaborationist" and was spreading its message "in northern Iraq through audiocassettes, communiqués and other means."[2]

In addition, a number of the major, traditionally conservative Kurdish tribes of Iraq had established a Kurdish Tribes Society in September 1991, in part because of their disapproval of the Kurdish Front's negotiations with Baghdad. This new group, also known as the "Conservatives Party" or the "Mosul Vilayet Council," was headed by Umar Agha (Turchi). It called for a democratic Iraq and sought contacts with Turkey, Saudi Arabia, Britain, and the United States.[3]

However, the Kurdish Front apparently has healed its own rifts caused by the Barzani-Talabani division over the negotiations with Baghdad. In January 1992 decisions were taken to attempt to unite all peshmerga fighters under a single command, establish a joint body to implement information and media affairs, and set up a unified taxation system. In addition, the Kurdish Front decided to halt the negotiations with Baghdad until it lifted the economic and administrative siege of the Kurdish-controlled area that had begun the previous October. Finally, the Front also decided to hold elections for a Kurdish national council or parliament and an overall leader whose title would be Leader of the Kurdish Liberation Movement in Iraqi Kurdistan. The consequences of such steps for the future of a united Iraq remained unclear, although the Front maintained that it favored a federal solution, rather than independence.

Although the elections held on May 19, 1992, failed to return a clear winner, the coalition government established subsequently by the KDP and the PUK has gone a long way toward creating a de facto Kurdish state protected by the United States and Turkey. This ironic situation would have been unthinkable before the 1991 Gulf War. Given Turkey's own serious Kurdish problem and its perceived need to keep the Iraqi Kurds friendly toward it and safe from Saddam, the de facto alliance between Turkey and the Iraqi Kurds is likely to continue. Indeed, it is distinctly possible that a de jure Kurdish state will eventually emerge in what is still northern Iraq. If it does, it will be largely because of the events set loose by the 1991 Gulf War.

Even if the Iraqi Kurds do not achieve statehood, however, an optimist might argue all sides have suffered and finally learned enough so that this time the Kurds, at least, will be given a meaningful autonomy that genuinely will satisfy them. This could be done within the framework of either a federal or unitary state that also will reassure the majority Arab population. While Saddam's record regarding the Kurds is appalling, over the years the Iraqi Kurds have been legally recognized and have been granted more cultural rights than in any other Middle Eastern country.

Although the pessimist might still maintain, given the failures in Iraq, that the only way to control the Kurds is to repress them, it is just possible that finally all the Iraqis will learn to respect and trust each other enough so that democracy can be established. The fact that such "impossible" visions have recently materialized in the former communist bloc—giving democracy a prestige it previously lacked—provides hope that it might begin to take root in Iraq too. Only time will tell.

The Kurdish prospects in Iraq, however, do not hinge merely on continuing tragedy or wishful thinking. One realistic avenue to pursue is for the United States to use the uniquely powerful position it still holds with its victory in the 1991 Gulf War and the collapse of the Soviet Union to promote democracy in Iraq.

The international community has never before been so aware of and taken such an interest in the Kurdish problem. The chances for an amelioration of the situation have not been better since the heady days of the March 1970 Manifesto and are not likely to be so good again for some time. If the United States can correctly blend carrot and stick, as it did in putting together the successful coalition against Saddam after August 1990, the states of the Middle East, including Iraq, are ready to be influenced. The United States should use its position of strength to help create a democratic Iraq in which the Kurds can live peacefully and have their basic human rights protected.

This will not be easy. The many problems encountered by the second Iraqi opposition conference that met in Vienna in June 1992 illustrate how difficult it will be to create a united, democratic Iraq. The Kurdish demand for federalism was opposed by many Shiite and Sunni groups at another Iraqi opposition meeting held under Kurdish auspices in northern Iraq during October. Moreover, the continuing U.N. sanctions against Saddam's regime threaten to lead to mass starvation, disease, and other social dislocations. What is more, the unstable situation of no war, no peace in northern Iraq invites a renewal of hostilities at any time with untold consequences. Despite its crushing defeat in the 1991 Gulf War, Baghdad's military remains vastly superior to anything the Kurds can muster. Only a continuing U.S. presence will deter a new Iraqi attack, but how long the United States will continue to provide this protection is unclear.

Certainly, however, Iraq possesses the prerequisites for economic success, as it is well endowed with both natural and human resources. Its more than 100 billion barrels of oil reserves are second only to that of Saudi Arabia, while the fertile land and fresh water supply in Iraq are the envy of the Arab world. In addition, the adult literacy rate and educational enrollment figures at all levels are high by Middle Eastern standards. With sound government, Iraq can soon regain the promise of a bright future Saddam so ignorantly threw away. Thus, despite the many remaining difficulties, there are also reasons to hope that the long tragedy of the Kurds in Iraq might finally end.

Notes

1. The Kurdish question in Iraq up to the 1970s and the fall of Mulla Mustafa Barzani in 1975 have already been well covered. See Edmund Ghareeb, *The Kurdish Question in Iraq* (Syracuse, NY: Syracuse University Press, 1981); Edgar O'Ballance, *The Kurdish Revolt, 1961–1970* (Hamden, CT: Archon Books, 1973); Sa'ad Jawad, *Iraq and the Kurdish Question, 1958–1970* (London: Ithaca Press, 1981); and Ismet Sheriff Vanly, "Kurdistan in Iraq," in *People without a Country: The Kurds and Kurdistan*, ed. Gerard Chaliand (London: Zed Press, 1980), pp. 153–210. A number of useful studies of the Kurds in general also exist. In particular, see Thomas Bois and Vladimir Minorsky, "Kurds, Kurdistan," *The Encyclopedia of Islam*, new ed., vol. 5, 1981, pp. 438–86; M. M. van Bruinessen, Agha, *Shaikh and State: On the Social and Political Organization of Kurdistan* (Utrecht: University of Utrecht, 1978); Gerard Chaliand, ed., *People without a Country: The Kurds and Kurdistan* (London: Zed Press, 1980); David McDowall, *The Kurds, Report no. 23* (London: Minority Rights Group Ltd., 1985); Nader Entessar, *Kurdish Ethnonationalism* (Boulder, CO: Lynne Rienner, 1992); Mehrdad Izady, *The Kurds: A Concise Handbook* (Washington, D.C.: Crane Russak, 1992); and Charles G. MacDonald, "The Kurdish Question in the 1980s," in *Ethnicity, Pluralism, and the State in the Middle East*, ed. Milton J. Esman and Itamar Rabinovich (Ithaca, NY: Cornell University Press, 1988), pp. 232–52.

2. No reliable estimates of the Kurdish population exist because most Kurds tend to exaggerate their numbers, while the states in which they live undercount them for political reasons. In addition, a significant number of Kurds have partially or fully assimilated into the larger Arab, Turkish, or Iranian populations surrounding them. Furthermore, debate continues whether such groups as the Lurs, Bakhtiyaris, Qashqais, Afshars, or Mamesanis are Kurds or not. Thus there is not even complete agreement on who is a Kurd. Nevertheless, a reasonable estimate is that there may be as many as 10 to 12 million Kurds in Turkey (18 to 21 percent of the population), 6 million in Iran (11 percent), 3.5 to 4 million in Iraq (20 to 23 percent), and 800,000 in Syria (7 percent). In 1974, before Barzani's final defeat and the subsequent population depletions through fighting, executions, and exile, the Kurds in Iraq probably represented as high as 26 percent of the total population.

3. All of this, of course, is not to deny that there were three great Kurdish revolts in modern Turkey, as well as a steadily escalating guerrilla insurgency there since 1984. For an analysis, see Michael M. Gunter, *The Kurdish Problem in Turkey: A Political Dilemma* (Boulder, CO: Westview

Press, 1990). In addition, the only Kurdish state to be established in the twentieth century was the short–lived Mahabad Republic in Iran following World War II. See William Eagleton, Jr., *The Kurdish Republic of 1946* (London: Oxford University Press, 1963); and Archie Roosevelt, Jr., "The Kurdish Republic of Mahabad," *Middle East Journal* 1 (July 1947), pp. 247–69.

4. On this point, see C. J. Edmonds, *Kurds, Turks and Arabs: Politics, Travel and Research in North–Eastern Iraq, 1919–1925* (London: Oxford University Press, 1957), p. 398.

5. Cited in Vanly, "Kurdistan in Iraq," p. 161.

6. Peter J. Beck, "A Tedious and Perilous Controversy: Britain and the Settlement of the Mosul Dispute, 1918–1926," *Middle Eastern Studies* 17 (April 1981), pp. 256–76. Also see Edmonds, *Kurds, Turks and Arabs*, for an earlier analysis.

7. Cited in Vanly, "Kurdistan in Iraq," p. 162. Also see Amir Hasanpour, "State Policy on the Kurdish Language: The Politics of Status Planning," *Kurdish Times* 4 (Summer–Fall 1991), pp. 42–63.

8. Stephen H. Longrigg, *Iraq, 1900 to 1950: A Political, Social, and Economic History* (London: Oxford University Press, 1953), p. 196.

9. Ibid., p. 328.

10. During the pro–Axis coup of Rashid Ali al–Gaylani in 1941, the shaikh once again escaped from house arrest and called for a Kurdish attack on the Arabs. Nothing came of this appeal, and Mahmud finally died on October 9, 1956.

NOTES 2

1. The following discussion is largely based on M. M. van Bruinessen, *Agha, Shaikh and State: On the Social and Political Organization of Kurdistan* (Utrecht: University of Utrecht, 1978), pp. 292–93, 329–31, and 346–48; Dana Adams Schmidt, *Journey Among Brave Men* (Boston: Little, Brown and Co., 1964), pp. 93–115; Hassan Arfa, *The Kurds: An Historical and Political Study* (London: Oxford University Press, 1966), pp. 117 ff.; William Eagleton, Jr., *The Kurdish Republic of 1946* (London: Oxford University Press, 1963), pp. 47–54; Stephen C. Pelletiere, *The Kurds: An Unstable Element in the Gulf* (Boulder, CO: Westview Press, 1984), pp. 96–99; C. J. Edmonds, "The Kurds and the Revolution in Iraq," *The Middle East Journal* 13 (Winter 1959), pp. 5–8; and a number of discussions with

knowledgeable Kurds. Although minor errors have undoubtedly crept in, I believe that the following picture is basically accurate.

2. Hanna Batatu, *The Old Social Class and the Revolutionary Movements of Iraq: A Study of Iraq's Old Landed and Commercial Classes and of its Communists, Ba'thists, and Free Officers* (Princeton, NJ: Princeton University Press, 1978), p. 43. For a further analysis of Kurdish religions, see Martin van Bruinessen, "Religion in Kurdistan," *Kurdish Times* 4 (Summer–Fall 1991), pp. 5–27.

3. Mark Sykes, *The Caliph's Last Heritage: A Short History of the Turkish Empire* (London: Macmillan and Co., Ltd., 1915), p. 561.

4. Ismet Sheriff Vanly, "Kurdistan in Iraq," in *People without a Country: The Kurds and Kurdistan*, ed. Gerard Chaliand (London: Zed Press, 1980), p. 158.

5. Barzani himself gave the following information about his religious education. See Schmidt, *Journey Among Brave Men*, p. 96.

6. Sa'ad Jawad, *Iraq and the Kurdish Question, 1958–1970* (London: Ithaca Press, 1981), p. 14.

7. Schmidt, *Journey Among Brave Men*, p. 96.

8. National Foreign Assessment Center (United States Central Intelligence Agency), *The Kurdish Problem in Perspective* (Aug. 1979), p. 37.

9. "Mustafa Barzani, Kurds' Leader Dies," *The New York Times,* Mar. 3, 1979, p. A13. The Kurds are notoriously vague about such details.

10. Eagleton, *Kurdish Republic of 1946*, p. 51.

11. Schmidt, *Journey Among Brave Men*, p. 93.

12. Ibid., p. 105.

13. This and the following citation were taken from Eagleton, *Kurdish Republic of 1946*, p. 51.

14. This and the following citations were taken from Schmidt, *Journey Among Brave Men*, pp. 197, 198–99, and 200.

15. Nauman M. al-Kanaani, *Limelight on the North of Iraq* (Baghdad: Dar al–Jumhuriya, 1965), pp. 66, 67, and 71.

16. See Arfa, *The Kurds*, p. 121.

17. The best source on the Mahabad Republic is Eagleton, *Kurdish Republic of 1946*. Also see the useful Archie Roosevelt, Jr., "The Kurdish Republic of Mahabad," *The Middle East Journal* 1 (July 1947), pp. 247–69.

18. Cited in Schmidt, *Journey Among Brave Men*, pp. 109–110. Other Kurdish observers, however, question some of Barzani's heroic claims.

19. After his release as an old man in the 1960s, Ahmad assumed a role as an intermediary between his younger brother, Mulla Mustafa, and Baghdad or his brother's Kurdish opponents. Although he never moved against Ahmad, Mulla Mustafa claimed that the older Barzani had "chosen the road of submission to the government and neutrality," and was "an old man who has been broken by twelve years in prison." Cited in ibid., pp. 202 and 268.

20. The following citations and much of the data were taken from ibid., pp. 110–13.

21. Later, however, after Nasser and Kassem had become enemies and Nasser had begun to flirt with supporting Barzani as a way to help reduce Kassem, the Egyptian leader pointed to a place in his office and declared to Barzani's delegates: "that is where Mullah Mustafa sat." Cited in ibid., p. 113.

22. The following list appears in Arfa, *The Kurds*, p. 134.

23. The following citations and data were taken from al-Kanaani, *Limelight on the North of Iraq*, pp. 68–70.

24. This and the following citation were taken from C. J. Edmonds, "The Kurds of Iraq," *The Middle East Journal* 11 (Winter 1957), p. 61.

25. This and the following citation were taken from Edmonds, "The Kurds and the Revolution in Iraq," pp. 4 and 8.

26. For analyses of this unique, transnational Arab party that was founded in Damascus in 1940 by Michel Aflaq, a Syrian Orthodox Christian intellectual, and Salah al–Din al–Baitar, a Sunni Muslim Syrian intellectual, see Kamel S. Abu Jaber, *The Arab Ba'th Socialist Party: History, Ideology, and Organization* (Syracuse, NY: Syracuse University Press, 1966); John Devlin, *The Baath Party: A History from Its Origins to 1966* (Stanford, CA: Hoover Institution Press, 1976); Majid Khadduri, *Socialist Iraq: A Study in Iraqi Politics Since 1968* (Washington, D.C.: The Middle East Institute, 1978); and Gordon Torrey, "The Baath Ideology and Practice," *The Middle East Journal* 23 (Autumn 1969), pp. 445–70. For further analyses of the Baath's position toward the Kurds, see Edmund Ghareeb, *The Kurdish Question in*

Iraq (Syracuse, NY: Syracuse University Press, 1981), pp. 45–86; and Jawad, *Iraq and the Kurdish Question*, pp. 222–76.

27. For the specifics of the "29 June Declaration," see Jawad, *Iraq and the Kurdish Question*, pp. 200–202.

28. Cited in ibid., p. 254.

29. The following text of the March 1970 Manifesto was taken from the publication of the Central Organ of the Iraqi Baath Party, *Settlement of the Kurdish Problem in Iraq: Discussion and Documents on the Peaceful and Democratic Settlement of the Problem* (Baghdad: Ath–Thawra Publications, [1974]), pp. 117–21, hereafter cited as *Settlement of the Kurdish Problem*. For partial texts of the Manifesto, see Khadduri, *Socialist Iraq*, pp. 231–40; and Vanly, "Kurdistan in Iraq," pp. 168–70.

30. The term *Nawroz* means "new sun" or "new day." It is celebrated annually on March 21, as the new year's day for the Kurds, Iranians, and other related peoples. In addition, for the Kurds Nawroz also symbolizes freedom because, according to one version of the legend, it was on that day that the blacksmith, Kawa, crushed the ruthless ruler, Zahhak, who had been feeding the brains of young men to two giant serpents' heads growing from his shoulders. The lighting of fires for Nawroz may be associated with the Kurds' probable Zoroastrian past.

31. Cited in David Adamson, The Kurdish War (New York: Praeger, 1965), p. 92.

32. Vanly, "Kurdistan in Iraq," p. 178.

33. For analyses of Saddam's usage of murder and terror, see Samir al-Khalil, *Republic of Fear: The Politics of Modern Iraq* (Berkeley: University of California Press, 1989); Middle East Watch, *Human Rights in Iraq* (New Haven: Yale University Press, 1990); Judith Miller and Laurie Mylroie, *Saddam Hussein and the Crisis in the Gulf* (New York: Times Books, 1990); and Efraim Karsh and Inari Rautsi, *Saddam Hussein: A Political Biography* (New York: The Free Press, 1991).

34. The following citations and analysis were taken from *Settlement of the Kurdish Problem*, pp. 123–65.

35. For the full text of the Algiers Accord and its later supplements, see Tareq Y. Ismael, *Iraq and Iran: Roots of Conflict* (Syracuse, NY: Syracuse University Press, 1982), pp. 60–68.

36. Cited in Mohammed H. Malek, "Kurdistan in the Middle East Conflict," *New Left Review*, no. 175 (1989), p. 86.

37. Cited in Ghareeb, *Kurdish Question in Iraq*, p. 155.

38. The following story was told to me by U.S. Ambassador William Eagleton, Jr., Washington, D.C., May 15, 1991. Other versions of Ubaidallah's demise exist, as facts concerning the Kurds are often elusive.

NOTES 3

1. For a thorough analysis of the ICP, see Hanna Batatu, *The Old Social Classes and the Revolutionary Movements of Iraq: A Study of Iraq's Old Landed and Commercial Classes and of Its Communists, Ba'athists, and Free Officers* (Princeton, NJ: Princeton University Press, 1978), pp. 367–1134. Also see Sa'ad Jawad, *Iraq and the Kurdish Question*, 1958–1970 (London: Ithaca Press, 1981), pp. 318–19, n. 67.

2. The following discussion is largely based on Jawad, *Iraq and the Kurdish Question*, pp. 13–14, 17, and 18–23; Hassan Arfa, *The Kurds: An Historical and Political Study* (London: Oxford University Press), pp. 120–24; Dana Adams Schmidt, *Journey Among Brave Men* (Boston: Little, Brown and Co., 1964), pp. 116–30; David McDowall, *The Kurds*, Report no. 23 (London: Minority Rights Group Ltd., 1985), p. 29; Martin van Bruinessen, "The Kurds Between Iran and Iraq," *Middle East Report*, no. 141 (July–August 1986), pp. 17–18 and 22–26; and my discussions with knowledgeable Kurds. Also see Chris Kutschera, *Le mouvement national kurde* (Paris: Flammarion, 1979); and Christiane More, *Les Kurdes aujourdhui: Mouvement national et partis politiques* (Paris: L'Harmattan, 1984).

3. Jawad, *Iraq and the Kurdish Question*, p. 20.

4. Schmidt, *Journey Among Brave Men*, p. 124.

5. Ibid., p. 125.

6. Ibid., p. 123.

7. Bruinessen, "The Kurds Between Iran and Iraq," p. 16. For an enlightening analysis of the diversity in Kurdish languages, see Mehrdad Izady, "A Kurdish Lingua Franca?" *Kurdish Times* 2 (Summer 1988), pp. 13–24, where the author declares that "the variations among them are as pronounced as, for example, those between Italian, Spanish, Catalan, and Portuguese." Ibid., p. 14.

8. Cited in Schmidt, *Journey Among Brave Men*, p. 204.

9. Cited in Bruinessen, "The Kurds Between Iran and Iraq," p. 22.

10. Cited in Edmund Ghareeb, *The Kurdish Question in Iraq* (Syracuse, NY: Syracuse University Press, 1981), p. 183.

NOTES 4

1. See Sa'ad Jawad, *Iraq and the Kurdish Question, 1958–1970* (London: Ithaca Press, 1981), pp. 278–88; Edmund Ghareeb, *The Kurdish Question in Iraq* (Syracuse, NY: Syracuse University Press, 1981), pp. 61; and Ismail al–Arif, *Iraq Reborn: A Firsthand Account of the July 1958 Revolution and After* (New York: Vantage Press, 1982), pp. 86–87.

2. This attempt at cooperation, however, was not built on firm historical foundations. Both the Ottoman and Persian empires had continuously intervened in Kurdish affairs in attempts to manipulate matters. The Kurds, for their part, had also participated willingly. See M. M. van Bruinessen, *Agha, Shaikh and State: On the Social and Political Organization of Kurdistan* (Utrecht: University of Utrecht, 1978), pp. 150–248. As to the effect on the Kurds of the Saadabad Treaty and Baghdad Pact, see Joyce Blau, *Le probleme kurde: Essai sociologique et historique* (Brussels: Centre pour l'Etude des Problemes du Monde Musulman Contemporain, 1963), p. 38. On the foreign policy of Iran during these years, see Ruhollah Ramazani, *The Persian Gulf: Iran's Role* (Charlottesville: University Press of Virginia, 1972); and Shahram Chubin and Sepehr Zabih, *The Foreign Relations of Iran: A Developing State in a Zone of Great–Power Conflict* (Berkeley: University of California Press, 1974).

3. This and the following data were taken from Thomas Powers, *The Man Who Kept the Secrets: Richard Helms and the CIA* (New York: Alfred A. Knopf, 1979), p. 130.

4. Cited in Dana Adams Schmidt, "The Kurdish Insurgency," *Strategic Review* 2 (Summer 1974), p. 54. Also see David Adamson, *The Kurdish War* (New York: Praeger, 1965), p. 94; and Lee Dinsmore, "The Forgotten Kurds," *The Progressive*, Apr. 1977, p. 39. Even earlier, in March 1945, the Heva Party had presented a memorandum to the U.S. ambassador in Iraq, Loy Henderson, reminding him of President Wilson's twelfth point concerning Kurdish self–determination and requesting American support for Kurdish autonomy. See Hassan Arfa, *The Kurds: An Historical and Political Study* (London: Oxford University Press, 1966), p. 125.

5. "The CIA Report the President Doesn't Want You to Read," *The Village Voice*, Feb. 16, 1976, pp. 70–92; hereafter cited as Pike Committee Report. The part dealing with Kurds is entitled "Case 2: Arms Support," and

appears on pp. 85 and 87–88. In addition, see the two essays William Safire wrote based on the Pike Committee Report: "Mr. Ford's Secret Sellout," *The New York Times*, Feb. 5, 1976, p. 31; and "Son of 'Secret Sellout,'" *The New York Times*, Feb. 12, 1976, p. 31.

6. According to the Pike Committee Report, it only amounted to "some $16 million."

7. According to the Pike Committee Report, these earlier proposals had been rejected (1) some time before August 1971, (2) in August 1971, and (3) in March 1972.

8. William Eagleton, Jr., letter to the author, dated July 10, 1991.

9. Henry Kissinger, *White House Years* (Boston: Little, Brown and Co., 1979), p. 1265.

10. Ibid.

11. Cited in Pike Committee Report.

12. Cited in Ghareeb, *The Kurdish Question in Iraq*, p. 140.

13. Pike Committee Report. The Forty Committee is an external bureaucracy in the executive branch of the United States government established to oversee covert operations and thus prevent abuses. See Edward Blaim, "Covert Action: Discussion," in *Intelligence Requirements for the 1990s: Collection, Analysis, Counterintelligence and Covert Action*, ed. Roy Godson (Lexington, KY: Lexington Books, 1989), p. 231.

14. This and the following citations were taken from the Pike Committee Report.

15. This and the following citations were taken from ibid.

16. Cited in Gwynne Roberts, "Kurdish Leader, Facing Possible Civil War, Looks to West for Support," *The New York Times*, Apr. 1, 1974, p. 14.

17. Cited in Ghareeb, *The Kurdish Question in Iraq*, p. 159.

18. Cited in the Pike Committee Report.

19. For a further discussion of these points, see Ismet Sheriff Vanly, "Kurdistan in Iraq," in *People without a Country: The Kurds and Kurdistan*, ed. Gerard Chaliand (London: Zed Press, 1980). pp. 189–92.

20. The following information was taken from Dan Raviv and Yossi Melman, *Every Spy a Prince: The Complete History of Israel's Intelligence Community* (Boston: Houghton Mifflin Company, 1990), pp. 21 and 82; and Ian Black and Benny Morris, *Israel's Secret Wars: A History of Israel's Intelligence Services* (New York: Grove Weidenfeld, 1991), pp. 184–85 and 327– 30. Also see Andrew Cockburn and Leslie Cockburn, *Dangerous Liaison: The Inside Story of the US–Israeli Covert Relationship* (New York: Harper Collins, 1991), pp. 104–105.

21. Jack Anderson, "Israelis Infiltrate Arab Regimes," *The Washington Post*, Sept. 17, 1972, p. B7.

22. Cited in Jason Morris, "Begin Airs Secret Israeli Aid to Kurds as Reminder for Iraqis," *The Christian Science Monitor*, Oct. 6, 1980, p. 11.

23. Jawad, *Iraq and the Kurdish Question*, p. 303.

24. Ghareeb, *The Kurdish Question in Iraq*, p. 133. Parastin was created in 1966.

25. Raviv and Melman, *Every Spy a Prince*, p. 428.

NOTES 5

1. Much of the relatively obscure data that appear in this chapter were garnered from interviews with various Kurdish sources who preferred to remain anonymous. Although some minor errors have undoubtedly crept in, I have been able to verify most of my facts and statements through various other sources.

2. Mamand had broken away from Talabani following the PUK's attack against the Barzani brothers' KDPPC in the spring of 1978.

3. Omar Sheikmous, "The Current Situation of the Kurds in Iraq," unpublished paper, June 1988, p. 1.

4. Ismet Sheriff Vanly, "Kurdistan in Iraq," in *People without a Country: The Kurds and Kurdistan*, ed. Gerard Chailiand (London: Zed Press, 1980), p. 178.

5. Clyde Haberman, "For Turkey and Kurds, Fragile Reconciliation," *The New York Times*, Nov. 3, 1989, p. 6; and "Minorities in the Gulf War," *Cultural Survival Quarterly* 11 (no. 4, 1987), p. 29.

6. Simande Siaband [Mehrdad Izady], "Mountains, My Home: An Analysis of

the Kurdish Psychological Landscape," *Kurdish Times 2* (Summer 1988), pp. 7, 9.

7. Vanly, "Kurdistan in Iraq," p. 196.

NOTES 6

1. For analyses of the ensuing struggle, see Anthony H. Cordesman and Abraham R. Wagner, *The Lessons of Modern War, vol. 2: The Iran–Iraq War* (Boulder, CO: Westview Press, 1990); Shahram Chubin and Charles Tripp, *Iran and Iraq at War* (Boulder, CO: Westview Press, 1988); Majid Khadduri, *The Gulf War: The Origin and Implications of the Iraq–Iran Conflict* (New York: Oxford University Press, 1988); Edgar O'Ballance, *The Gulf War* (London: Brassey's Defence Publishers, 1988); Christopher Joyner, ed., *The Persian Gulf War: Lessons for Strategy, Law, and Diplomacy* (New York: Greenwood Press, 1990); and Charles Davis, ed., *After the War: Iraq, Iran and the Arab Gulf* (Chichester: Carden Publications, 1990).

2. The following analysis is based, in part, on Martin van Bruinessen, "The Kurds Between Iran and Iraq," *Middle East Report*, no. 141 (July–August 1986), pp. 14–27; David McDowall, *The Kurds*, Report no. 23 (London: Minority Rights Group Ltd., 1985), pp. 24–25; Malcolm Yapp, "'The Mice Will Play'": Kurds, Turks and the Gulf War," in *The Gulf War: Regional and International Dimensions*, ed. Hanns W. Maull and Otto Pick (New York: St. Martin's Press, 1989), pp. 109–15; Charles G. MacDonald, "The Impact of the Gulf War on the Iraqi and Iranian Kurds," *Middle East Contemporary Survey*, 7 (1982–83), pp. 261–72; Ali-Fuat Borovali, "Kurdish Insurgencies, the Gulf War, and Turkey's Changing Role," *Conflict Quarterly* 7 (Fall 1987), pp. 29–45; Mohammed H. Malek, "Kurdistan in the Middle East Conflict," *New Left Review*, no. 175 (1989), pp. 87–94; and Nader Entessar, "The Kurdish Mosaic of Discord," *Third World Quarterly* 11, no. 4 (1989), pp. 95–98.

3. Cited in *Tercuman* (Turkey), Oct. 10, 1986, p. 7.

4. Although population statistics are woefully inadequate here, one estimate indicates that the Turkomans constitute approximately 220,000, or less than 2 percent, of the Iraqi population, while the Assyrians, who are Christians, number maybe 133,000, or less than 1 percent. See Helen Chapin Metz, ed., *Iraq: A Country Study* (Washington, D.C.: Government Printing Office, 1990), p. 86.

5. Omar Sheikmous, "The Current Situation of the Kurds in Iraq," unpublished paper, June 1988, p. 3.

6. "Kurds Use Gulf War to Pursue Own Interests of Independence," *The Age*, Jan. 4, 1988.

7. Cited in Judith Vidal–Hall, "War of the Mountain Men," *South*, May 1987, pp. 14–15.

8. See Patrick E. Tyler, "Kurds Posing Threat for Iraq Backed by Iran: They Destabilize the Northern Front," *International Herald Tribune*, Feb. 20–21, 1988.

9. Judith Vidal-Hall, "The Gulf's Other War," *South*, October 1986, p. 18.

10. Hazhir Teimourian, "Kurds Burn Hussein Palace," *The Sunday Times*, Jan. 31, 1988.

11. The following citations were taken from Hazhir Teimourian, "Iraq's Kurds Talk About Breaking Away," *Jerusalem Post*, Mar. 23, 1988.

12. Sheikmous, "The Current Situation of the Kurds in Iraq," p. 4.

13. Anthony Hyman, *Elusive Kurdistan: The Struggle for Recognition*, Conflict Study no. 214 (London: The Centre for Security and Conflict Studies, 1988), p. 14.

14. See, in general, Michael M. Gunter, *The Kurds in Turkey: A Political Dilemma* (Boulder, CO: Westview Press, 1990).

15. For details, see Sam Cohen, "Turkey's Mysterious Strike in Iraq Underlines Ongoing Effort to Uproot Kurdish Nationalism," *Christian Science Monitor*, July 14, 1983, p. 12; "Terrorist Attacks in Eastern Turkey," *Briefing* (Turkey), Oct. 15, 1984, pp. 11–12; "Turks Bomb Kurdish Rebel Camp," *The Armenian Weekly*, Aug. 30, 1986, p. 3; and "Turkish Warplanes Raid Kurdish Guerrilla Bases in Iraq," *The Armenian Mirror-Spectator*, Mar. 14, 1987, pp. 1, 3.

16. "Kurds Killed in Turkish Air Raid on Guerrilla Hide–outs in Iraq," *Financial Times*, Aug. 21, 1986.

17. This and the following statements were cited in "Turks Said Showing New Resolve to Put Down Rebellion by Kurdish Separatists; Kurds Strike," *The Armenian Reporter*, Sept. 11, 1986, p. 1.

18. The following discussion is based, in part, on Suha Bolukbasi, "Turkey Copes with Revolutionary Iran," *Journal of South Asian and Middle Eastern Studies* 13 (Fall/Winter 1989), pp. 102–106; Sam Cohen, "Gulf War Worries Turkey," *Christian Science Monitor*, Oct. 30, 1986, p. 9, 10; Elaine Sciolino, "Turks Warn Iran on Cutting Pipeline," *The New York Times*,

Mar. 16, 1987, p. A3; "Iranian Guards Stage Mini–invasion of Turkey," *Insight*, Sept. 28, 1987, p. 37; Martin Seiff, "Kurdish Gains in Mideast Seen as Threat to Iraq and Turkey," *The Washington Times*, Sept. 7, 1987; Borovali, "Kurdish Insurgencies, the Gulf War, and Turkey's Changing Role," pp. 37–42; and Bruinessen, "The Kurds Between Iran and Iraq," pp. 14–27.

19. On Iraq's usage of chemical warfare, see Valerie Adams, *Chemical Warfare, Chemical Disarmament* (Bloomington: Indiana University Press, 1990), pp. 85–90; and Edward M. Spiers, *Chemical Weaponry: A Continuing Challenge* (New York: St. Martin's Press, 1989), pp. 121–25. See also Middle East Watch, *Human Rights in Iraq* (New Haven, CT: Yale University Press, 1990), pp. 75–85.

20. Sheikmous, "The Current Situation of the Kurds in Iraq," pp. 3–4.

21. Hyman, *Elusive Kurdistan*, p. 14.

22. James Bone, "Genocide of Kurds," *The Daily Telegraph*, Mar. 4, 1988.

23. The following analysis is based on United States Congress, Senate, Committee on Foreign Relations and House Committee on Foreign Affairs, *Country Reports on Human Rights Practices for 1988*, 101st Cong., 1st sess., 1989, pp. 1355–56; Patrick E. Tyler, "Iran Charges Iraq with a Gas Attack and Its Grisly Toll," *International Herald Tribune*, Mar. 24, 1988; Jim Muir, "Iraqi Gas Attacks Revive Horrors of the Great War," *The Times*, Mar. 27, 1988; and Alan Cowell, "Iran–Iraq Tactics: Fighting for Political Advantage," *International Herald Tribune*, Mar. 24, 1988.

24. United States Congress, Country Reports 1988, p. 1356. Also see United States Congress, Senate, Committee on Foreign Relations, *Chemical Weapons Use in Kurdistan: Iraq's Final Offensive*, a staff report by Peter W. Galbraith and Christopher Van Hollen, Jr., 100th Cong., 2d sess., Sept. 21, 1988, where it is concluded that "overwhelming evidence exists that Iraq used chemical weapons on Kurdish civilians in a major offensive in northern Iraq that began August 25, 1988."

25. Physicians for Human Rights, "Medical Team Finds Evidence of Iraqi Use of Chemical Weapons on Kurds," press release, Oct. 22, 1988.

26. United States Congress, Senate, "Proceedings and Debates of the 102d Congress, First Session," *Congressional Record*, vol. 137, no. 10, Jan. 15, 1991.

27. Cited in "A Good-Will Gesture: But at What Cost?" *Briefing* (Turkey), Sept. 12, 1988, p. 4.

28. Cited in "A Warm Welcome to the Peshmerges," *Briefing*, Sept. 5, 1988, p. 4. For a negative portrayal of the Turkish role, see Vera Beaudin Saeedpour, "From the Lion to the Fox: Iraqi Kurdish Refugees in Turkey," *Kurdish Times* 3 (Fall 1990), pp. 17–23.

29. Cited in "Ankara Concerned Over Increased Foreign Interest in Kurds," *Briefing*, Sept. 19, 1988, p. 6.

30. The following discussion is largely based on Tim Kelsey, "Cold Cuts Down Refugee Kurds on Turkish Border," *The Independent*, Oct. 12, 1988; Hugh Pope, "Kurdish Refugees Face Catastrophe as Winter Arrives," *The Washington Times*, Oct. 10, 1988; and "Kurds Stone Kurds Trying to Go Home," *The Washington Times*, Oct. 6, 1988.

31. Clyde Haberman, "How the Kurds Are Cared For: 7 Months in Tents," *The New York Times*, Mar. 31, 1989, p. A4.

32. Ibid.

33. Tim Kelsey, "Turkey Accused of Smuggling Kurds to Iran," *The Independent*, July 19, 1989.

34. Jim Bodgener, "Turkey Denies 'Dumping' Kurdish Refugees," *Financial Times*, July 20, 1989.

35. This citation and the following data were taken from Vera Beaudin Saeedpour, "Insidious Intent: The Destruction and Depopulation of Iraqi Kurdistan," briefing paper presented to the United States Congressional Human Rights Caucus, Oct. 20, 1989, pp. 3–4. For further discussions of Iraq's relocation policy, see Middle East Watch, *Human Rights in Iraq*, pp. 85–92; and Sheri Lazier, *Into Kurdistan: Frontiers under Fire* (London: Zed Books Ltd., 1991), pp. 102–104.

36. This and the following citation were taken from the Kurdistan Popular Democratic Party (KPDP), "On the Deportation of Iraqi Kurds from Iraq," Apr. 7, 1982.

37. It is surprising, therefore, that no Kurds showed up in southern Iraq when the allied forces occupied the area at the end of the 1991 War. Earlier reports had indicated that relocated Kurds had been permitted to return to their homes in northern Iraq during the first stages of the Iran–Iraq War.

38. Cited in Michael Siegert, "Two Millions in Concentration Camps," *Vienna Profil*, Jan. 7, 1991, pp. 34–35; as cited in *Foreign Broadcast Information Service—Near East & South Asia*, Jan. 8, 1991, p. 28.

39. United States Congress, *Country Reports* 1988, p. 1360.

40. The following discussion largely is based on Patrick E. Tyler, "Iraq Targets Kurds for Relocation," *The Washington Post,* Apr. 30, 1989, p. A34; Hazhir Teimourian, "Iraq Army Forces 100,000 Kurds to Leave Big Town," *The Times,* June 14, 1989; Tim Kelsey, "Resettled Kurds Mourn Lost Mountains," *The Independent,* Aug. 19, 1989; Edward Mortimer, "Iraq Troops Begin Forcibly Resettling 300,000 Kurds," *Financial Times,* June 3, 1989; and Victoria Brittain, "Iraq Troop Crackdown on Kurdish Nationalists," *The Guardian,* May 22, 1989.

41. "Eight Thousand Civilian Kurds Have Disappeared in Iraq, What Has Happened To Them?" Report by a Preparatory Committee, Jawad Mella, Secretary General, London, Nov. 1987.

42. This and the following citation and analysis are based on Amnesty International News Release, "Amnesty International Says Hundreds Reported Executed in Iraq Aged from 14 to 73," Feb. 25, 1988; and "Baghdad Accused of Torturing Children," *The Times,* Mar. 13, 1988. For a wide–ranging analysis of other human rights violations against the Iraqi Kurds, see Middle East Watch, *Human Rights in Iraq,* pp. 69–96, 145–50.

43. Amnesty International News Release, "Amnesty International Calls on Iraqi Government to Investigate Reports of Security Forces' Use of Thallium Poisoning Against Political Opponents," Jan. 13, 1988.

NOTES 7

1. Cited in Suzanne Goldenberg, "Kurds Would Not Fight Iraq," *The Guardian,* Nov. 27, 1990.

2. This and the following citations were taken from Najm Abdal al–Karim, "Talabani Tells Al-Majallah: We Would Fight Alongside Arab Forces to Liberate Kuwait!" *Al-Majallah,* Dec. 19–24, 1990; as cited in *Foreign Broadcast Information Service—Near East & South Asia,* Jan. 4, 1991, p. 39; hereafter cited as *FBIS-NES.*

3. Cited in Elaine Sciolino, "Kurds: Stateless People with a 70–Year Grudge," *The New York Times,* Mar. 27, 1991, p. A6.

4. Cited in Olivia Ward, "Silent Nightmare of Kurds May Return to Haunt Saddam's Chemical Warriors," *The Toronto Star,* Sept. 2, 1990.

5. Cited in Jonathan C. Randal, "Kurdish Rebels Weigh Attack," *International Herald Tribune,* Jan. 25, 1991.

6. Cited in "Kurdish Leader Predicts Saddam's Collapse," *Vienna Die Presse*, Jan. 23, 1991, p. 6; as cited in *FBIS-NES*, Jan. 24, 1991, p. 28.

7. This and the following citation were taken from Lucian O. Meysels, "Interview with Jalal Talabani . . . ," *Vienna Wochenpresse*, Apr. 11, 1991, pp. 28–29; as cited in *FBIS-NES*, Apr. 16, 1991, p. 25.

8. William Safire, "Remember the Kurds," *The New York Times*, Jan. 28, 1991, p. A23.

9. Harvey Morris, "Kurds Set to Strike If Saddam's Rule Ends," *The Independent*, Jan. 29, 1991.

10. "Behind the News," Damascus Syrian Arab Television Network in Arabic, 1918 GMT, Mar. 24, 1991; as cited in *FBIS-NES*, Mar. 26, 1991, p. 26.

11. Cited in "Kurdish Leader Jalal Talabani Interviewed," *London Keyhan*, Mar. 7, 1991, p. 12; as cited in *FBIS-NES*, Mar. 20, 1991, p. 63. These troops were the josh, not Iraqi regulars.

12. Cited in Jonathan C. Randal, "Kurdish Commander Invites Saddam Foes to Meeting in Iraq," *Washington Post*, Mar. 27, 1991, p. A25.

13. (Clandestine) Voice of the People of Kurdistan in Arabic, 1745 GMT, Mar. 20, 1991; as cited in *FBIS-NES*, Mar. 21, 1991, p. 15.

14. Cited in Lisa Beyer, "Getting Their Way," *Time*, Apr. 1, 1991, p. 34.

15. The following data were taken from Judith Miller, "Iraqi Dissidents Preparing for Rule If Hussein Topples," *The New York Times*, Mar. 22, 1991, p. A8.

16. This and the following citation were taken from Alex Efty, "Rebels Hold North Iraq: Army Forces Claim South," *The Tennessean*, Mar. 27, 1991, p. A–6.

17. "Kurdish Leader on Significance of Talks in Ankara," Ankara Anatolia in English, 1515 GMT, Mar. 14, 1991; as cited in *FBIS- NES*, Mar. 15, 1991, p. 39.

18. Ibid.

19. "Kurdish Leader Wants 'Democratic Regime,'" Ankara Anatolia in Turkish, 1415 GMT, Mar. 31, 1991; as cited in *Foreign Broadcast Information Service—West Europe*, Apr. 1, 1991, p. 33; hereafter cited as *FBIS-WEU*.

20. The following analysis is largely based on "Talabani Affair Overshadows Soviet Tour on Eve of US Talks," *Briefing* (Turkey), Mar. 18, 1991, pp. 3–7;

and "Free Debate in Ankara But Death and Injury Elsewhere," *Briefing*, Mar. 25, 1991, pp. 5–6.

21. This and the following citation were taken from Tayfun Talipoglu, "Ozal Reassures Commanders Against Kurdish State," *Milliyet*, Mar. 26, 1991, p. 19; as cited in *FBIS-WEU*, Apr. 1, 1991, p. 27.

22. "Rebels Admit Government Has Upper Hand in Irbil," (Clandestine) Voice of Rebellious Iraq in Arabic, 0615 GMT, Apr. 3, 1991; as cited in *FBIS-NES*, Apr. 3, 1991, p. 14.

23. "Kurdish Leader on United States 'Green Light' to Saddam," Paris AFP in English, 1645 GMT, Mar. 28, 1991; as cited in *FBIS- NES*, Mar. 29, 1991, p. 12.

24. This and the following citation were taken from "Kurds Appeal for Help: Face Saddam Counterattack," Paris AFP in English, 1545 GMT, Mar. 28, 1991; as cited in *FBIS-NES*, Mar. 29, 1991, p. 12.

25. Lucian O. Meysels, "A Shame for the Entire World," *Vienna Wochenpresse*, Apr. 11, 1991, pp. 28–29; as cited in *FBIS-NES*, Apr. 16, 1991, p. 25.

26. Michael Wines, "Iraqi Revolts Ebb as Kurdish Rebels Flee to Borders," *The New York Times*, Apr. 3, 1991, p. A6.

27. This and the following citations were taken from Michael R. Gordon (with Eric Schmitt), "Much More Armor Than United States Believed Fled Back to Iraq," *The New York Times*, Mar. 25, 1991, p. A1.

28. This and the following citation were taken from Patrick E. Tyler, "Schwarzkopf Says Truce Enabled Iraqis to Escape," *The New York Times*, Mar. 27, 1991, p. A7.

29. "Saddam Will Not Survive," Der Spiegel, Mar. 25, 1991, pp. 214–17; as cited in *FBIS-NES*, Mar. 26, 1991, p. 28.

30. Cited in "United States Turns Down Plea to Intervene as Kirkuk Falls," *International Herald Tribune*, Mar. 30, 1991.

31. Meysels, "A Shame for the Entire World."

32. Jim Drinkard, "Bush Reportedly Gave Secret Orders to Aid Rebels in Iraq," *Cookeville Herald-Citizen*, Apr. 3, 1991, p. 1; and Clifford Krauss, "Baker Aide Talks with Iraqi Dissidents in United States," *The New York Times*, Apr. 4, 1991, p. A6.

33. See United States Congress, Senate, Committee on Foreign Relations, *Civil War in Iraq: A Staff Report to the Committee on Foreign Relations, United States Senate*, by Peter W. Galbraith, 102d Cong., 1st sess., May 1991.

34. "Kurds Head for Mountains under Withering Iraqi Fire, *The Tennessean*, Apr. 2, 1991, p. 4-A.

35. "Only Unused United States Refugee Aid Said Acceptable," Tehran IRNA in English, 1000 GMT, May 2, 1991; as cited in *FBIS-NES*, May 2, 1991, p. 27.

36. "State of Emergency Governor Discusses Refugees," Ankara Domestic Service in Turkish, 2000 GMT, Apr. 22, 1991; as cited in *FBIS-WEU*, Apr. 23, 1991, p. 56.

37. Turhan Dede, "The Iraqi Refugee Catastrophe," *The Turkish Times*, Apr. 15, 1991, p. 11.

38. This and the following citation were taken from "Ozal Proposes Kurdish Camps in North Iraq," Ankara TRT Television Network in Turkish, 1700 GMT, Apr. 16, 1991; as cited in *FBIS-WEU*, Apr. 17, 1991, p. 29.

39. "Governor Estimates 400,000 Iraqi Refugees," Ankara Anatolia in English, 1600 GMT, Apr. 11, 1991; as cited in *FBIS-WEU*, Apr. 12, 1991, p. 37.

40. Arslan Bulut, "Cyprus and Beyond," *Tercuman*, Apr. 16, 1991, p. 6; as cited in *FBIS-WEU*, Apr. 23, 1991, p. 57.

41. Cited in "Iran Leader Blames United States and Iraq for Deaths, Disaster and Refugees," *The New York Times*, Apr. 13, 1991, p. 4.

42. Michael Wines, "United States May Send More to Kurds in Iran," *The New York Times*, Apr. 30, 1991, p. A5.

43. The connotation given by the term "safe havens" implied more of a human-itarian purpose and less of a restriction of Iraqi territorial integrity than that of "enclaves."

44. "Foreign Minister Denounces West's Move on Kurds," Baghdad INA in Arabic, 1716 GMT, May 1, 1991; as cited in *FBIS-NES*, May 2, 1991, p. 8.

45. "Paper Calls United States Presence `Illegitimate,'" Baghdad INA in Arabic, 0650 GMT, Apr. 29, 1991; as cited in *FBIS-NES*, Apr. 29, 1991, p. 17.

46. Cited in George J. Church, "Mission of Mercy," *Time*, Apr. 29, 1991, p. 41. Bush's explanation ignored, however, the situation of the Kurdish refugees

in Iran, as well as the pressure put on him by his Turkish ally to return them home.

47. Youssef M. Ibrahim, "Iraq Rejects European Plan for Kurdish Haven in North," *The New York Times*, Apr. 10, 1991, p. A6.

48. For the text of this Resolution, see "UN Security Council Resolution 688 on Repression of Iraqi Civilians," *US Department of State Dispatch*, Apr. 8, 1991. pp. 233–34.

49. See Princeton N. Lyman, "Update on Iraqi Refugees and Displaced Persons," *US Department of State Dispatch*, May 27, 1991, p. 379.

50. Michael Kelly, "Back to the Hills," *The New Republic*, June 3, 1991, p. 23.

NOTES 8

1. This and the following citations and information were taken from "Further on Government–Kurdish Talks," Paris AFP in English, 1745 GMT, Apr. 19, 1991; as cited in *Foreign Broadcast Information Service—Near East & South Asia*, Apr. 22, 1991, p. 26; hereafter cited as *FBIS-NES*. Also see the report that Saddam had offered to negotiate as early as March 29, on the bases of the March 1970 Manifesto, in Martin Woollacott, "Kurds Struggle to Recapture Strategic Kirkuk," *The Guardian*, Mar. 30, 1991.

2. This and the following dates must be considered approximations as the various announcements made by the two sides are not always exactly in agreement.

3. See Jean Gueyras, "Interview with Iraqi Communist Party Politburo Member Fakhri Karim," *Le Monde*, Aug. 9, 1991, p. 4; as cited in *FBIS-NES*, Aug. 14, 1991, p. 12.

4. The following citation and analysis are taken from "Talabani News Conference," Amman Domestic Service in Arabic, 0400 GMT, Apr. 25, 1991; as cited in *FBIS-NES*, Apr. 25, 1991, pp. 13–14; and "Talabani Comments on Talks with Regime on Accord," London BBC Television Network in English, 2130 GMT, May 1, 1991; as cited in *FBIS-NES*, May 8, 1991, p. 15.

5. This and the following citations were taken from "Kurdish Leader on Demands Made at Baghdad Talks," Paris AFP in English, 0555 GMT, Apr. 23, 1991; as cited in *FBIS-NES*, Apr. 23, 1991, p. 16.

6. This and the following citation were taken from "Saddam, Barzani Discuss Baghdad Agreement," Berlin ADN in German, 1409 GMT, May 11, 1991; as cited in *FBIS-NES*, May 17, 1991, p. 16.

7. This and the following citations were taken from "Holds News Conference 18 May," Baghdad INA in Arabic, 0800 GMT, May 18, 1991; as cited in *FBIS-NES*, May 20, 1991, pp. 18–20.

8. This and the following citations were taken from "Barzani on Autonomy Meeting with Saddam," Baghdad INA in Arabic, 0915 GMT, May 21, 1991; as cited in *FBIS-NES*, May 21, 1991, p. 7.

9. The following citations and discussion are largely based on "Holds News Conference 18 May," as cited in *FBIS-NES*, May 20, 1991, pp. 18–20.

10. The following citations came from "Barzani Tells Sa'd Salih Jabr: Kurdish People Made Sacrifices Alone," *London Al-Sharq Al-Awsat in Arabic*, May 1, 1991, pp. 1, 4; as cited in *FBIS-NES*, May 3, 1991, p. 17.

11. The following citations were taken from "Text of an Open Appeal from a Number of Iraqi Opposition Leaders to the Kurdish Movement Leaders in Iraq," (Clandestine) Voice of Iraqi Opposition in Arabic, 1500 GMT, May 9, 1991; as cited in *FBIS-NES*, May 10, 1991, pp. 13–14.

12. "Groups Urge Barzani to Close 'Loophole,'" (Clandestine) Voice of Iraqi Opposition in Arabic, 1300 GMT, Apr. 27, 1991; as cited in *FBIS-NES*, Apr. 29, 1991, p. 12.

13. "Muhammad Sadiq al-Husayni Dispatch from Tehran," Paris Radio Monte Carlo in Arabic, 1720 GMT, May 19, 1991; as cited in *FBIS-NES*, May 20, 1991, p. 20.

14. Cited in Pat Fry, "Iraqi Opposition Condemns Talks with Hussein," *Peoples Weekly World*, May 4, 1991, p. 5.

15. Cited in Manfred Quiring, "The Immoral Fraternal Kiss," *Berliner Zeitung*, Apr. 27–28, 1991, p. 2; as cited in *FBIS-NES*, Apr. 29, 1991, p. 73.

16. "Interview with Barzani," Mainz ZDF Television Network in German, 1730 GMT, June 21, 1991; as cited in *FBIS-NES*, June 25, 1991, p. 15.

17. The following was taken from "'Text' of Autonomy Draft Law for Kurdistan," *London Al-Sharq Al-Awsat in Arabic*, June 29, 1991, p. 6; as cited in *FBIS-NES*, July 3, 1991, pp. 17–21.

18. "Talabani Says Talks with Saddam to Last Months," (Clandestine) Voice of Iraqi Opposition in Arabic, 1300 GMT, June 12, 1991; as cited in *FBIS-NES*, June 13, 1991, p. 12.

19. "Talabani: 'Obstacles' Remain Regarding Autonomy," (Clandestine) Voice of Iraqi Opposition in Arabic, 1300 GMT, June 16, 1991; as cited in *FBIS-NES*, June 17, 1991, p. 12.

20. Seyhmus Cakan, "A Cautious Approach by Jalal Talabani," *Milliyet*, June 27, 1991, p. 9; as cited in *FBIS-NES*, July 2, 1991, p. 15.

21. This and the following citation were taken from Kamran Qurrah Daghi, "Kurds Reject Baghdad's Conditions," *London Al-Hayah*, June 29, 1991, pp. 1, 4; as cited in *FBIS-NES*, July 3, 1991, p. 21.

22. "Barzani Says Accord 'Still Imminent,'" Paris AFP in English, 1512 GMT, July 1, 1991; as cited in *FBIS-NES*, July 2, 1991, p. 17.

23. Bulent Ecevit and Derya Sazak, "Interview with Saddam Hussein," *Milliyet*, May 29, 1991, p. 11; as cited in *FBIS-NES*, May 31, 1991, p. 18.

24. This and the following citations and discussion were taken from Ibrahim Mawwar, "Kurdish Leaders' Return to Baghdad Postponed: Disagreements over 'Commitments' Flare Up," *London Al-Sharq Al-Awsat*, June 29, 1991, pp. 1, 4; as cited in *FBIS-NES*, July 3, 1991, pp. 22–23.

25. Cited in Ufuk Tekin, "Kurds Have Been Unable to Agree with Saddam Hussein," *Cumhuriyet*, July 1, 1991, p. 9; as cited in *FBIS-NES*, July 3, 1991, p. 15.

26. Nawwar, "Kurdish Leaders Return to Baghdad Postponed," as cited in *FBIS-NES*, July 3, 1991, p. 22.

27. Daghi, "Kurds Reject Baghdad's Conditions," as cited in *FBIS-NES*, July 3, 1991, p. 22.

28. Cited in Kamran Qurrah Daghi, "Barzani and Talabani Decide to Delay Agreement with Baghdad," *London Al-Hayah*, June 27, 1991, pp. 1, 7; as cited in *FBIS-NES*, July 1, 1991, p. 18.

29. Nawwar, "Kurdish Leaders Return to Baghdad Postponed," as cited in *FBIS-NES*, July 3, 1991, p. 22.

30. Daghi, "Kurds Reject Baghdad's Conditions," as cited in *FBIS-NES*, July 3, 1991, p. 21.

31. "Comments on Agreement with Government," Baghdad INA in Arabic, 0745 GMT, July 15, 1991; as cited in *FBIS-NES*, July 15, 1991, p. 28.

32. "Terms Saddam Meeting 'Positive,'" Baghdad INA in Arabic, 0655 GMT, July 14, 1991; as cited in *FBIS-NES*, July 15, 1991, p. 28.

33. Ibid.

34. "Barzani on Agreement, 'Riots' in North," Baghdad INA in Arabic, 1726 GMT, July 19, 1991; as cited in *FBIS-NES*, July 22, 1991, p. 13.

35. "Barzani on Events in North, Autonomy Agreement," Baghdad INA in Arabic, 0735 GMT, July 22, 1991; as cited in *FBIS-NES*, July 22, 1991, p. 14.

36. "Turkey Sets Ground Rules for 'Poised Hammer,'" *Briefing*, July 29, 1991, p. 9.

37. "Barzani on Agreement, 'Riots' in North," as cited in *FBIS-NES*, July 22, 1991, p. 14.

38. "Negotiations with Kurds Reportedly Faltering," Paris Radio Monte Carlo in Arabic, 1700 GMT, July 17, 1991; as cited in *FBIS-NES*, July 18, 1991, p. 17.

39. "Kurdish Source Says Baghdad Talks at 'Dead End,'" Paris AFP in English, 0605 GMT, Sept. 9, 1991; as cited in *FBIS-NES*, Sept. 9, 1991, p. 17.

40. "Rebel Leaders to Meet, Discuss Negotiations," (Clandestine) Voice of Iraqi Opposition in Arabic, 1300 GMT, Aug. 24, 1991; as cited in *FBIS-NES*, Aug. 26, 1991, p. 23.

41. Vedat Venerer, "Exclusive Interview with Mahmud Osman," *Cumhuriyet*, Aug. 28, 1991, p. 10; as cited in *FBIS-NES*, Sept. 4, 1991, p. 54.

42. Zubeyir Kindira, "Saddam Husayn Has Besieged Karkuk," *Gunaydin*, Sept. 2, 1991, p. 8; as cited in *FBIS-NES*, Sept. 6, 1991, p. 4.

43. "Kurdish Source Says Baghdad Talks at 'Dead End,'" as cited in *FBIS-NES*, Sept. 9, 1991, p. 17.

44. "Jalal Talabani Addresses Irbil Masses 29 Aug.," (Clandestine) Voice of the People of Kurdistan in Arabic, 1705 GMT, Sept. 1, 1991; as cited in *FBIS-NES*, Sept. 3, 1991, p. 26.

45. "Major Turkish Operation in Northern Iraq: Turkish Kurdish Guerrilla Camps Destroyed," *Neue Zuercher Zeitung* (International Edition), Aug. 9, 1991, pp. 1–2; as cited in *Foreign Broadcast Information Service—West Europe*, Aug. 22, 1991, p. 45; hereafter cited as *FBIS-WEU*.

46. Cited in Ihsan Dortkardes, "We Don't Object to the Operation," *Hurriyet*, Aug. 11, 1991, p. 18; as cited in *FBIS-WEU* Aug. 14, 1991, p. 39.

47. Ankara Anatolia in English, 0900 GMT, Aug. 13, 1991; as cited in *FBIS-WEU*, Aug. 14, 1991, p. 38.

48. Barcin Yinanc, "Exclusive Interview with Jalal Talabani," *Milliyet*, Aug. 11, 1991, p. 16; as cited in *FBIS-WEU*, Aug. 14, 1991, p. 38.

49. "ARGK, PKK Leaders Interviewed on Events," *2000 Ikibin'e Dogru*, Aug. 18, 1991, pp. 12–15; as cited in *FBIS-WEU*, Aug. 21, 1991, p. 41.

50. Abdullah Ocalan, "The Outlook for Political Struggle and the Autonomy Talks in Southern Kurdistan," *Serxwebun*, July 1991, pp. 1, 7–11; as cited in *FBIS-WEU*, Aug. 29, 1991, p. 42.

51. Vedat Yenerer, "Exclusive Interview with Mahmud Osman," as cited in *FBIS-WEU*, Sept. 4, 1991, p. 54.

52. Ibid., p. 55.

53. (Clandestine) Voice of Iraqi Kurdistan in Arabic, 1655 GMT, Oct. 27, 1991; as cited in *FBIS-NES*, Oct. 28, 1991, p. 14.

54. Cited in "Demirel in Serious Commitment and Warning," *Briefing*, Dec. 16, 1991, p. 10.

Notes 9

1. Inis L. Claude, Jr., *Swords into Plowshares: The Problems and Progress of International Organization*, 4th ed. (New York: Random House, 1971), p. 247.

2. For analyses of the theory and problems of collective security, see ibid., pp. 245–85; Inis L. Claude, Jr., *Power and International Relations* (New York: Random House, 1962), pp. 94–204; and Ernst B. Haas, "Types of Collective Security: An Examination of Operational Concepts," *American Political Science Review* 49 (March 1955), pp. 40–62.

3. Claude, *Swords into Plowshares*, p. 254.

4. Larry L. Fabian, *Soldiers without Enemies: Preparing the United Nations for Peacekeeping* (Washington, D.C.: The Brookings Institution, 1971), p. 16. For further analyses, see James M. Boyd, *United Nations Peace-Keeping Operations: A Military and Political Appraisal* (New York: Praeger, 1971); Leon Gordenker and Thomas G. Weiss, *Soldiers, Peacekeepers and Disasters* (Riverside, CA: Macmillan, 1991); Indar J. Rikhye, *The Theory and Practice of Peacekeeping* (London: C. Hurst and Co., 1984); and United Nations Department of Public Information, *The Blue Helmets: A Review of United Nations Peacekeeping* (New York: United Nations, 1985).

5. When President Nasser of Egypt told UNEF (the U.N. peacekeeping force in Egypt) to leave in 1967, for example, UNEF did, despite the knowledge that such an action would probably remove the last remaining barrier to war against Israel. (And war did ensue.)

6. British forces have long participated in the U.N. peacekeeping force in Cyprus (UNFICYP) because they were already there under treaty rights that brought Cyprus independence in 1960.

7. Cited in *UN Chronicle*, June 1991, p. 9.

8. *UN Chronicle*, Sept. 1991, p. 16.

9. For the complete text of this Resolution, see "UN Security Council Resolution 688 on Repression of Iraqi Civilians," *US Department of State Dispatch*, Apr. 8, 1991, pp. 233–34. The Resolution was adopted by a vote of 10 to 3 (Cuba, Yemen, and Zimbabwe) with 2 abstentions (China and India).

10. Cited in *UN Chronicle*, Sept. 1991, p. 16.

11. U.N. Doc. A/46/612, Nov. 4, 1991, p. 1.

12. Ibid.

13. "Memorandum of Understanding Signed on 18 April 1991," contained as an "Enclosure" in U.N. Doc. S/22663, May 31, 1991, pp. 2–4.

14. "Annex [Concerning the Deployment of a U.N. Guards Contingent]," contained in ibid., pp. 6–7.

15. This and the following data were taken from "Humanitarian Assistance to Iraqi Refugees and Displaced Persons: Report of the Secretary–General," U.N. Doc. A/46/612, Nov. 4, 1991, pp. 1–9.

16. Ibid.

17. Ibid.

18. See, for example, John G. Stoessinger, *Financing the United Nations System* (Washington, D.C.: The Brookings Institution, 1964); and A. Leroy Bennett, *International Organizations: Principles and Issues*, 5th ed. (Englewood Cliffs, NJ: Prentice–Hall, 1991), pp. 89–95.

19. The following data and figures were taken from Princeton L. Lyman, "Crisis of Refugees and Displaced Persons in Iraq," *US Department of State Dispatch*, Apr. 22, 1991, p. 274.

20. U.N. Doc. A/46/612, Nov. 4, 1991, p. 2.

21. "Humanitarian Assistance in Iraq," *US Department of State Dispatch*, Jan. 13, 1992, p. 26. The Red Cross provided another $100 million. Melinda L. Kimble, "Humanitarian Situation in Iraq," *US Department of State Dispatch*, Mar. 23, 1992, p. 223.

22. BBC World Report, June 30, 1992.

23. Cited in U.N. Doc. A/46/612, Nov. 4, 1991, p. 2.

24. This and the following citation were taken from ibid.

Notes 10

1. "Talabani on Negotiation with Baghdad," *London Saut Al-Kuwayt in Arabic*, June 14, 1992, p. 14; as cited in *Foreign Broadcast Information Service— Near East & South Asia*, June 17, 1992, p. 19; hereafter cited as *FBIS-NES*.

2. Cited in "Barzani Issues Press Communique at End of Visit," (Clandestine) Voice of Iraqi Kurdistan in Arabic, 1820 GMT, Feb. 25, 1992; as cited in *Foreign Broadcast Information Service—West Europe*, Feb. 27, 1992, p. 25; hereafter cited as *FBIS-WEU*.

3. This and the following data and citations are taken from Kanan Makiya, "The Anfal: Uncovering an Iraqi Campaign to Exterminate the Kurds," *Harper's Magazine*, May 1992, p. 61. Makiya earlier wrote an analysis of Saddam under the pseudonym, Samir al–Khalil, *The Republic of Fear: The Politics of Modern Iraq* (Berkeley: University of California Press, 1989). See Chapter 6 for an analysis of other atrocities of Baghdad against the Kurds.

4. Makiya, "The Anfal," p. 53.

5. Ibid.

6. Ibid., p. 54.

7. Cited in ibid., p. 58.

8. This and the following citations and data were taken from Chris Hedges, "Kurds' Dream of Freedom Slipping Away," *The New York Times*, Feb. 6, 1992, p. A1, A10.

9. Cited in "Barzani Cited on Disputes within Kurdistan Front," *London Al-Hayah*, Dec. 22, 1991, p. 5; as cited in *FBIS-NES*, Jan. 3, 1992, p. 25.

10. Cited in "Talabani Interviewed on Elections, Unity," Paris Radio Monte Carlo in Arabic, 1725 GMT, May 16, 1992; as cited in *FBIS-NES*, May 18, 1992, p. 19.

11. "PUK Delegation Visits Tehran; Battles in South," Paris Radio Monte Carlo in Arabic, 1700 GMT, Mar. 28, 1992; as cited in *FBIS-NES*, Mar. 30, 1992, p. 22.

12. The following analysis is based on Leslie Weaver, "Iraqi Kurds Prepare for First Free Elections," *The New York Times*, May 15, 1992, p. A14; and "Barzani—Elections Should End Militia Rule," Paris AFP in English, 0725 GMT, Feb. 2, 1992; as cited in *FBIS-NES*, Feb. 6, 1992, p. 18.

13. By this formula, simple mathematics would indicate that the Kurdish Front believed there were approximately 3,150,000 people under their jurisdiction in northern Iraq. A month later the Kurds were allocated twenty–two out of eighty–seven seats in the interim government committee formed by the Iraqi opposition in Vienna on the basis of their proportion of the total Iraqi population. This figure indicates that just over 25 percent of the Iraqi population was Kurdish.

14. On June 8, 1992, shortly after the smaller parties failed to receive the required minimum of 7 percent of the vote to receive seats in the parliament, a further unification was announced between these two parties and the KPDP of Sami Rahman. The Kurdish Socialist Party (PASOK) was referred to as the Kurdistan Democratic Independence Party. Thus it would seem that there were now only six members of the Iraqi Kurdistan Front. The elections had helped begin a process of unification.

15. Ismet G. Imset, "Further Reportage on Kurdistan Elections," *Turkish Daily News*, May 8, 1992, pp. 1, 12; as cited in *FBIS-NES*, May 19, 1992, p. 19.

16. Mahmut Bulut, "Turkoman Leader Discusses Kurdish Elections," *Istanbul Turkiye*, Apr. 9, 1992, p. 5; as cited in *FBIS-NES*, Apr. 23, 1992, p. 23.

17. Cited in Aziz Atkan, "Kurds Exclude Turkomans from Elections," *Istanbul Hurriyet*, Apr. 12, 1992, p. 15; as cited in *FBIS-NES*, Apr. 21, 1992, p. 22.

18. This and the following citation were quoted in "'Covenant' Pledges Respect for Results," (Clandestine) Voice of the People of Kurdistan in Arabic, 1703 GMT, May 17, 1992; as cited in *FBIS-NES*, May 18, 1992, p. 20.

19. "Kurds to Form 'All–Party' Governing Coalition," Paris AFP in English, 0620 GMT, May 21, 1992; as cited in *FBIS-NES*, May 21, 1992, p. 15.

20. Ibid., p. 16.

21. "Elections Deadlocked, 2d Poll Set," Paris AFP in English, 1810 GMT, May 22, 1992; as cited in *FBIS-NES*, May 26, 1992, p. 11.

22. "Parties to Share Assembly 'Equally,'" Paris AFP in English, 2325 GMT, May 22, 1992; as cited in *FBIS-NES*, May 20, 1992, p. 11.

23. (Clandestine) Voice of the Iraqi People in Arabic, 1400 GMT, May 27, 1992; as cited in *FBIS-NES*, May 28, 1992, p. 24.

24. "Parties to Share Assembly 'Equally'"; as cited in *FBIS-NES*, May 20, 1992, p. 11.

25. This and the following citations were taken from "Barzani, Talabani Agree to Cooperate," (Clandestine) Voice of Iraqi Kurdistan in Arabic, 1535 GMT, May 23, 1992; as cited in *FBIS-NES*, May 26, 1992, p. 12.

26. "Talabani Interviewed on Kurdistan Elections," *London Sawt Al-Kuwayt Al-Duwali*, June 13, 1992, p. 5; as cited in *FBIS-NES*, June 19, 1992, p. 23.

27. This and the following citations were taken from "Turkish Paper Interviews Barzani," *Istanbul 2000 Ikibin'e Dogru*, May 31, 1992, p. 13; as cited in *FBIS-NES*, June 9, 1992, p. 26.

28. "Assembly Speaker on Kurdish Elections," *Baghdad Alif Ba'*, May 27, 1992, p. 6; as cited in *FBIS-NES*, June 3, 1992, p. 19.

29. "Turkish Paper Interviews Barzani"; as cited in *FBIS-NES*, June 9, 1992, p. 26.

30. "PUK Leader Talabani Interviewed," *Istanbul 2000 Ikibin'e Dogru*, May 31, 1992, pp. 10–12; as cited in *FBIS-NES*, June 9, 1992, p. 27.

31. This and the following citations were taken from "Kurds' Barzani Discusses Peace Efforts, Autonomy," (Clandestine) Voice of Iraqi Kurdistan in Arabic, 1653 GMT, Apr. 13, 1992; as cited in *FBIS-NES*, Apr. 15, 1992, p. 41.

32. "Kurdish Parties Announce Unity, Form Leadership," (Clandestine) Kurdistan Voice of Unification in Arabic, 1738 GMT, June 21, 1992; as cited in *FBIS-NES*, June 22, 1992, p. 29.

33. This and the following citations and data were taken from "Turkish Paper on Nascent Kurdish State," *Istanbul 2000 Ikibin'e Dogru*, May 31, 1992, pp. 8–18; as cited in *FBIS-NES*, June 8, 1992, p. 27.

34. This and the following data were garnered from P. V. Vivekanand, "Kurds Said Exporting Oil to Turkey," *Amman Jordan Times*, Apr. 21, 1992, p. 7; as cited in *FBIS-NES*, Apr. 21, 1992, p. 18.

35. Ibid., p. 19.

36. U.S. Department of State Dispatch, Mar. 23, 1992, p. 224.

37. This and the following citations were taken from "Report Details Cross–Border Trade with Iraq," *Turkish Daily News*, May 30, 1992, p. 3; as cited in *FBIS-WEU*, June 5, 1992, p. 41.

38. "Kurdistan National Council Meets 20 Jun[e]," (Clandestine) Voice of Iraqi Kurdistan in Arabic, 1450 GMT, June 21, 1992; as cited in *FBIS-NES*, June 22, 1992, p. 29.

39. "Kurdish Council Holds Meeting, Elects Speaker," (Clandestine) Voice of Iraqi Kurdistan in Arabic, 1445 GMT, June 4, 1992; as cited in *FBIS-NES*, June 4, 1992, p. 13.

40. "Kurdistan Council of Ministers Named," (Clandestine) Voice of the People of Kurdistan in Arabic, 1712 GMT, July 4, 1992; as cited in *FBIS-NES*, July 6, 1992, p. 46.

41. This and the following citations were taken from "Expectations from New Kurdish Cabinet Noted," (Clandestine) Voice of the Kurdistan Revolution Radio in Arabic, 1718 GMT, July 6, 1992; as cited in *FBIS-NES*, July 9, 1992, p. 29. 42. The first had been held in Beirut in March 1991.

43. "Al-Da'wah Criticizes Conference," *Beirut Al-Safir*, June 20, 1992, p. 12; as cited in *FBIS-NES*, June 22, 1992, p. 27.

44. "Tension in Opposition Reported," (Clandestine) Voice of the Iraqi People in Arabic, 1400 GMT, June 19, 1992; as cited in *FBIS-NES*, June 22, 1992, p. 25.

Notes 11

1. *Milliyet*, no. 1636, Aug. 31, 1930; as cited in Kendal [Nezan], "Kurdistan in Turkey," in *People without a Country: The Kurds and Kurdistan*, ed. Gerard Chaliand (London: Zed Press, 1980), p. 65. For background analyses, see Michael M. Gunter, *The Kurds in Turkey: A Political Dilemma* (Boulder. CO: Westview Press, 1990); and Michael M. Gunter, "The Kurdish Problem in Turkey," *The Middle East Journal* 42 (Summer 1988), pp. 389–406.

2. Article 26 of the present (1982) Turkish Constitution.

3. "Demirel Warns on Effects of Kurdish Issue," *Cumhuriyet*, Mar. 26, 1991, p. 4; as cited in *Foreign Broadcast Information Service—Western Europe*, Apr. 2, 1991, pp. 36–37; hereafter cited as *FBIS-WEU*.

4. "Unbanning of Kurdish Discussed, Examined," *Nokta*, Feb. 10, 1991, pp. 26–27; as cited in *FBIS-WEU*, Mar. 6, 1991, p. 29.

5. Ilter Sagirsoy, "No, Despite Ozal," *Nokta*, Feb. 24, 1991, pp. 28–29; as cited in *FBIS-WEU*, Mar. 26, 1991, pp. 41–42.

6. "Ozal Puts Up Brave Performance in Strasbourg—But Brussels Still Says 'No,'" *Briefing* (Ankara), Oct. 2, 1989, p. 4.

7. Muserref Seckin and Ilter Sagirsoy, "Measures to Solve Kurdish Problem Proposed," *Nokta*, June 3, 1990, pp. 17–22; as cited in *FBIS-WEU*, Aug. 6, 1990, p. 38.

8. Sevket Okant and Murat Bardacki, "We Met with Abdullah Ocalan," *Hurriyet*, Apr. 1, 1990, p. 16; as cited in FBIS-WEU, Apr. 9, 1990, p. 26.

9. "The Southeast Report: What Does It Say?" *Briefing*, July 23, 1990, p. 5.

10. Helsinki Rights Watch, *Destroying Ethnic Identity: The Kurds of Turkey, An Update* (New York: Helsinki Rights Watch, 1990), pp. 13–18. Also see Martin van Bruinessen, "The Kurds in Turkey: Further Restrictions of Basic Rights," *International Commission of Jurists: The Review*, no. 45 (1990), pp. 46–52.

11. Sefik Kahramankaptan, "The Issue of Protecting the Kurds," *Tempo*, Feb. 2, 1991, pp. 16–17; as cited in *FBIS-WEU*, Feb. 22, 1991, p. 37.

12. Ilter Sagirsoy and Nedret Ersamel, "We Created 10 Million Kurds," *Nokta*, Feb. 10, 1991, pp. 20–27; as cited in *FBIS-WEU*, Mar. 6, 1991, p. 26.

13. "Reasons for Change Elaborated," Ankara Anatolia in English, 1510 GMT, Jan. 28, 1991; as cited in *FBIS-WEU*, Jan. 29, 1991, p. 56.

14. The following citations are taken from Institut Kurde de Paris, *Information and Liaison Bulletin*, no. 70, Jan. 1991, pp. 2–4; and "Language Freedom to Herald Democracy Drive?" *Briefing*, Feb. 11, 1991, pp. 6–9.

15. Sagirsoy and Ersanel, "We Created 10 Million Kurds," as cited in *FBIS-WEU*, Mar. 6, 1991, p. 27.

16. Mehmet Korkmaz, "Reactions from Kurdish Intellectuals," *Tempo*, Feb. 3–9, 1991, pp. 14–15; as cited in *FBIS-WEU*, Mar. 7, 1991, p. 37.

17. "Good-for-You to Ozal from Kurds," *Nokta*, Feb. 17, 1991, pp. 26–29; as cited in *FBIS-WEU*, Mar. 26, 1991, pp. 39–41.

18. Mehmet Ali Birand, "Interview with Abdullah Ocalan," *Milliyet*, Mar. 25, 1991, p. 19; as cited in *FBIS-WEU*, Apr. 2, 1991, p. 39.

19. "Kurdish Rebel Leader Proposes Talks with Ankara," Paris AFP in English, 0333 GMT, Mar. 23, 1991; as cited in *FBIS-WEU*, Mar. 25, 1991, pp. 44–45.

20. The following discussion and citations were taken from "Nationalist Uproar Spreads After Oath–Taking Incident," *Briefing*, Nov. 11, 1991, pp. 3–6.

21. Ihsan Akdemir, "Restoration in Southeast," *Milliyet*, Dec. 2, 1991, p. 17; as cited in *FBIS-WEU*, Jan. 8, 1991, p. 58.

22. Cited in Meric Koyatasi, "Demirel on Domestic, Foreign Policy, Cyprus," *Hurriyet*, Nov. 26, 1991, p. 18; as cited in *FBIS-WEU*, Dec. 3, 1991, p. 46.

23. Kamran Qurrah Daghi, "Deputy Premier Inonu Explains Policy on Kurds," *London Ali-Hayah*, Dec. 13, 1991, p. 4; as cited in *FBIS-WEU*, Dec. 17, 1991, p. 57.

24. Cited in "Coalition Outlines Plans for Southeast," *Milliyet*, Nov. 17, 1991, p. 16; as cited in *FBIS-WEU*, Dec. 18, 1991, pp. 55–56.

25. Ibid., p. 55.

26. "Kurdish Reality Recognized," Ankara Anatolia in English, 1505 GMT, Dec. 8, 1991; as cited in *FBIS-WEU*, Dec. 9, 1991, p. 55.

27. This and the following citation were taken from "The Kurdish Question: From 1991 to 1992," *Briefing*, Jan. 6, 1992, pp. 9–10.

28. Ismet G. Imset, "Report on PKK, Dev Sol Camps in Lebanon," *Turkish Daily News,* Dec. 4, 1991, pp. 8, 11; as cited in *FBIS-WEU*, Dec. 18, 1991, p. 53.

29. "Part Two of Interview," *Turkish Daily News*, Nov. 26, 1991, p. 5; as cited in *FBIS-WEU*, Dec. 3, 1991, p. 56.

30. "Demirel Comments on PKK, German Ties," Ankara TRT Television Network in Turkish, 1700 GMT, Mar. 30, 1992; as cited in *FBIS-WEU*, Mar. 31, 1992, p. 25.

31. "SDPP Reports Set to Embarrass Leadership and Government," *Briefing*, Apr. 13, 1992, p. 6.

32. Helsinki Watch, "Kurds Massacred: Turkish Forces Kill Scores of Peaceful Demonstrators," vol. 4, no. 9 (June 1992), p. 14.

33. Caroline Moorehead, "'Secret War' Against Kurds in Turkey," *The Independent*, Jan. 20, 1992.

34. Ismet G. Imset, "Terrorist Acts in Southeast Detailed," *Turkish Daily News*, May 27, 1992, p. 3; as cited in *FBIS-WEU*, June 15, 1992, p. 42.

35. Ali Ozluer, "The PKK Has Declared War," *Istanbul Hurriyet*, Mar. 24, 1992, p. 19; as cited in *FBIS-WEU*, Apr. 1, 1992, p. 39.

36. "Warplanes Strafe Sirnak, PKK's Ocalan Comments," Paris AFP in English, 1650 GMT, Mar. 24, 1992; as cited in *FBIS-WEU*, Mar. 25, 1992, p. 44.

37. "Milliyet Interviews PKK Leader Ocalan, Part II," *Istanbul Milliyet*, Mar. 24, 1992, p. 14; as cited in *FBIS-WEU*, Mar. 27, 1992, p. 42.

38. "Milliyet Interviews PKK Leader Ocalan, Part I," *Istanbul Milliyet*, Mar. 23, 1992, p. 14; as cited in *FBIS-WEU*, Mar. 27, 1992, p. 42.

39. "Milliyet Interviews PKK Leader Ocalan, Part II," as cited in *FBIS-WEU*, Mar. 27, 1992, p. 43.

40. "Milliyet Interviews PKK Leader Ocalan, Part III," as cited in *FBIS-WEU*, Mar. 27, 1992, p. 44.

41. Donald L. Horowitz, *Ethnic Groups in Conflict* (Berkeley: University of California Press, 1985), p. 683.

42. Ibid., p. 684.

43. "Ozal on Syrian Aid to 'Terrorist Groups,'" *London Al-Hayah*, Dec. 15, 1991, p. 5; as cited in *FBIS-WEU*, Dec. 18, 1991, p. 42.

44. This and the following citation appeared in "Military and Assembly to Agree to Protection of Some Kurds," *Briefing*, June 22, 1992, p. 9.

45. "Learning to Live with 'Kurdistan,'" *Briefing*, June 1, 1992, p. 11.

46. "Ankara OKs Emergency Law But Crisis Only Deepens in SE," *Briefing*, June 29, 1992, p. 15.

47. Cited in "Iraqi Kurds Reportedly to Block Terrorist Attacks," Ankara TRT Television Network, 1600 GMT, Apr. 8, 1992; as cited in *FBIS-WEU*, Apr. 9, 1992, p. 43.

48. "Talabani Calls on PKK 'To End Armed Action,'" Ankara Anatolia in Turkish, 1415 GMT, Oct. 18, 1991; as cited in *FBIS-WEU*, Oct. 21, 1991, p. 58.

49. This and the following citation were taken from "Meets with Demirel," Ankara TRT Television Network in Turkish, 1600 GMT, June 9, 1992; as cited in *FBIS-WEU*, June 11, 1992, p. 42.

50. "Barzani Arrives, Criticizes PKK 'Savagery,'" Ankara Radyolari Network in Turkish, 2000 GMT, Mar. 30, 1992; as cited in *FBIS-WEU*, Mar. 31, 1992, p. 27.

51. "Spokesman Comments on Barzani Request for Aid," Ankara Anatolia in Turkish, 1515 GMT, Apr. 1, 1992; as cited in *FBIS-WEU*, Apr. 2, 1992, p. 41.

52. "DPK Lodges Protest Over Turkish Air Raids," *Turkish Daily News*, June 2, 1992, p. 2; as cited in *FBIS-WEU*, June 9, 1992, p. 40.

53. Ibid., p. 41.

54. Cited in "Barzani Reassures Turkey on Elections," Paris AFP in English, 1815 GMT, May 17, 1992; as cited in *Foreign Broadcast Information Service—Near East & South Asia*, May 18, 1992, p. 21; hereafter cited as *FBIS-NES*.

55. This and the following data were taken from Ismet G. Imset, "PKK: The Deception of Terror (Countering Stability in Turkey), Part II," *Briefing* (Supplement), June 6, 1988, p. 20.

56. "On Elections, PKK, Independence," *Istanbul Milliyet*, Feb. 23, 1992, p. 7; as cited in *FBIS-WEU*, Feb. 26, 1992, p. 26.

57. This and the following citation appear in Imset, "PKK: Deception of Terror."

58. "A Good–Will Gesture: But at What Cost?" *Briefing*, Sept. 12, 1988, p. 6.

59. "Will the PKK Be a Regional Issue?" *Briefing*, Mar. 14, 1988, p. 11.

60. "Talabani's Meeting with PKK Leader Reported," *Istanbul Hurriyet*, Dec. 22, 1991, p. 16; as cited in *FBIS-WEU*, Dec. 27, 1991, p. 12.

61. "Formation of PKK–Affiliated Party Reported," *Istanbul Cumhuriyet*, Nov. 1, 1991, p. 10; as cited in *FBIS-WEU*, Dec. 18, 1991, p. 55.

62. Cited in "Talabani Calls on PKK 'To End Armed Action.'"

63. "PKK Said to Suspend Armed Activity Until March," *Gunaydin*, Nov. 28, 1991, p. 8; as cited in *FBIS-WEU*, Dec. 3, 1991, p. 50.

64. Ismet G. Imset, "PKK Promises No More Military Attacks," *Turkish Daily News*, Dec. 10, 1991, pp. 1, 11; as cited in *FBIS-WEU*, Dec. 16, 1991, p. 42.

65. Ismet G. Imset, "Further on Interview," *Turkish Daily News*, Nov. 28, 1991, p. 5; as cited in *FBIS-WEU*, Dec. 5, 1991, p. 40.

66. Ismet G. Imset, "Cease–Fire Announcement Causing PKK 'Confusion,'" *Turkish Daily News*, Dec. 19, 1991, pp. 1, 11; as cited in *FBIS-WEU*, Dec. 26, 1991, p. 25.

67. This and the following citation were taken from "PKK's Ocalan on Turkish, U.S., Syrian Policies," *Istanbul 2000 Ikibin'e Dogru*, Mar. 22, 1992, pp. 18–29; as cited in *FBIS-WEU*, Apr. 23, 1992, p. 28.

68. This and the following citations were taken from ibid., p. 29.

69. Cited in "Talabani Comments on Ankara, Talks, PKK," *Turkish Daily News*, June 16, 1992, p. 2; as cited in *FBIS-WEU*, June 29, 1992, p. 54.

70. "Talabani: Iraq 'Preparing for War Against Turkey,'" Ankara TRT Television Network, 1600 GMT, June 14, 1992; as cited in *FBIS-WEU*, June 15, 1992, p. 39.

71. "DPK Political Bureau Criticizes PKK, Ankara," (Clandestine) Voice of the Iraqi People in Arabic, 1700 GMT, Mar. 25, 1992; as cited in *FBIS-NES*, Mar. 26, 1992, p. 15.

72. "PKK Denounces Barzani as 'Collaborator,'" *Istanbul Hurriyet*, Feb. 24, 1992, p. 14; as cited in *FBIS-WEU*, Feb. 28, 1992, p. 44.

73. This and the following citation were taken from "Ocalan Said to Order Deaths of Barzani, Talabani," *Istanbul Tercuman*, Jan. 24, 1992, p. 11; as cited in *FBIS-WEU*, Jan. 27, 1992, p. 43.

74. This and the following citations were garnered from "Ocalan Interviewed on Foreign Support for PKK," *Istanbul Milliyet*, Mar. 26, 1992, p. 14; as cited in *FBIS-WEU*, Mar. 30, 1992, p. 36.

75. "PKK Survey: Impact of Rural Violence," *Briefing*, Aug. 17, 1987, p. 6–7.

76. "Turkey's Kurds and the Gulf War," *Mid East Markets*, Jan. 25, 1988.

77. "Iraq Reportedly Supplies PKK with Firearms," *Istanbul Tercuman*, Oct. 14, 1991, p. 12; as cited in *FBIS-WEU*, Oct. 18, 1991, p. 45.

78. Cited in Chris Hedges, "Iraq, in Retaliatory Move, Is Now Arming Turkish Kurds," *International Herald Tribune*, Oct. 21, 1991.

79. "PUK Leader Urges PKK Dialogue with Turkey," *Istanbul Hurriyet*, Oct. 19, 1991, p. 20; as cited in *FBIS-WEU*, Oct. 24, 1991, p. 26.

80. Cited in "Kurdish Socialist Leader Seeks Turkoman Ties," *Turkish Daily News*, May 4, 1992, p. 3; as cited in *FBIS-NES*, May 11, 1992, p. 21.

81. This and the following data were taken from Atilla Korkmaz, "PKK Camp Established Near Mosul," *Istanbul Hurriyet*, June 6, 1992, p. 18; as cited in *FBIS-WEU*, June 16, 1992, p. 43.

82. This and the following citation were taken from Ismet G. Imset, "Exclusive Interview with Jalal Talabani," *Turkish Daily News*, June 16, 1992, p. 2; as cited in *FBIS-WEU*, June 24, 1992, p. 54.

83. This and the following citation were taken from ibid., p. 53.

84. Nilufer Yalcin, "Secret Meeting Between Saddam Husayn and Abdullah Ocalan," *Istanbul Milliyet*, July 1, 1992, p. 13; as cited in *FBIS-WEU*, July 9, 1992, p. 42.

85. "Final Installment of Saddam Husayn Interview," *Istanbul Hurriyet*, Feb. 13, 1992, p. 7; as cited in *FBIS-NES*, Feb. 14, 1992, p. 28.

86. "Paper Scores 'Double Standard' on Turkish Kurds," Baghdad INA in Arabic, 0740 GMT, Mar. 10, 1992; as cited in *FBIS-NES*, Mar. 11, 1992, p. 16.

Notes 12

1. Ismet G. Imset, "Kurdish Workers Party Leader Discusses Issues," *Turkish Daily News*, Nov. 27, 1991, p. 5; as cited in *Foreign Broadcast Information Service—Western Europe*, Dec. 5, 1991, p. 37; hereafter cited as *FBIS-WEU*. Abdullah Ocalan, the leader of the PKK, claimed that the PAK "is a political party which has been influenced by the ideological and political perspective of the PKK and adapted according to South Kurdistan." Ibid.

2. Cited in Yasemin Congar, "New Organization from PKK," *Istanbul Cumhuriyet*, Nov. 1, 1991, p. 10; as cited in *FBIS-WEU*, Dec. 18, 1991, p. 54.

3. Stephen C. Pelletiere has argued that the influence of Barzani and Talabani is "overrated" and that the real power among the Iraqi Kurds is held by aghas or traditional landlords. See his *The Kurds and Their Agas: An Assessment of the Situation in Northern Iraq* (Carlisle Barracks, PA: Strategic Studies Institute, 1991), pp. v, 24. Although these traditional elements remain important, based on the analysis in this book, it is clear that Pelletiere has overrated their power.

Selected Bibliography

For numerous, additional references to specific articles in newspapers, the reader should refer to the notes at the end of each chapter.

TRANSLATION SERVICES

Foreign Broadcast Information Service—Near East & South Asia. Referred to as *FBIS-NES,* Jan. 1991–.

Foreign Broadcast Information Service—West Europe. Referred to as *FBIS-WEU,* Jan. 1991–.

INTERVIEWS

Eagleton, William, Jr. Former United States Ambassador to Syria. Washington D.C., May 1991.

Ghareeb, Edmund. Authority on the Iraqi Kurds. Washington, D.C., Nov. 1991.

Izady, Mehrdad. Authority on the Kurds. New York, Aug. 1991.

Partowmah, Mozaffer. Spokesman of the Islamic Party of Kurdistan (PIK). Washington, D.C., Nov. 1991.

Saeedpour, Vera Beaudin. Director, Kurdish Library. New York, May 1991.

Salih, Barham. Repreesentative of the Iraqi Kurdistan Front and the Patriotic Union of Kurdistan. Washington, D.C., Nov. 1991.

Smothers Bruni, Mary Ann. Journalist who travelled in northern Iraq in the summer of 1991. Washington, D. C., Nov. 1991.

Vanly, Ismet Sheriff. Kurdish academician. Toronto, Canada, Nov. 1989.

CORRESPONDENCE

Eagleton, William, Jr. Former United States Ambassador to Syria. July 10, 1991.

DOCUMENTS
United States

National Foreign Assessment Center (United States Central Intelligence Agency). *The Kurdish Problem in Perspective.* Aug. 1979.

United States Congress. Senate. Committee on Foreign Relations. *Chemical Weapons Use in Kurdistan: Iraq's Final Offensive.* A staff report by Peter W. Galbraith and Christopher Van Hollen, Jr., 100th Cong., 2d sess., Sept. 21, 1988.

―――. *Civil War in Iraq: A Staff Report to the Committee on Foreign Relations, United States Senate.* By Peter W. Galbraith, 102d Cong., 1st sess., May 1991.

―――. Senate, Committee on Foreign Relations, and House, Committee on Foreign Affairs. *Country Reports on Human Rights Practices for 1988,* 101st Cong., 1st sess., 1989.

IRAQI

Kanaani, Nauman M. al–. *Limelight on the North of Iraq.* Baghdad: Dar al-Jumhuriya, 1965.

Thawra, ath–. (Central Organ of the Baath Party). *Settlement of the Kurdish Problem in Iraq: Discussion and Documents on the Peaceful and Democratic Settlement of the Problem.* Baghdad: Ath–Thawra Publications, [1974].

KURDISH PUBLICATIONS AND DOCUMENTS

Al Karadaghi, Mustafa. "The Role that Kurds Played in the Ancient World." *Kurdistan Times* No. 1 (Winter 1990), pp. 25– 51.

―――. "Kurdish Language." *Kurdistan Times* No. 1 (Winter 1990), pp. 52–65.

Baker, Chahin. "The Kurdish Question and the Lack of Outside Support." *Kurdish Times* 1 (Spring 1986), pp. 27–32.

Bruinessen, Martin van. "Religion in Kurdistan." *Kurdish Times* 4 (Summer-Fall 1991), pp. 5–27.

Hasanpour, Amir. "State Policy on the Kurdish Language: The Politics of Status Planning." *Kurdish Times* 4 (Summer-Fall), pp. 42–85.

Homer, Kak. "The Mockery of the Kurdish Autonomous Region." *Kurdistan Times* No. 1 (Winter 1990), pp. 130–39.

Institut Kurde de Paris. *Information and Liaison Bulletin.* 1983–.

Izady, Mehrdad. "A Kurdish Lingua Franca?" *Kurdish Times* 2 (Summer 1988), pp. 13–24.

———. "Persian Carrot and Turkish Stick." *Kurdish Times 3* (Fall 1990), pp. 31–47.

———. "The Question of an Ethnic Identity: Problems in the Historiography of Kurdish Migrations and Settlements." *Kurdish Times* 1 (Summer 1986), pp. 16–18.

"Kurdistan: A Forgotten Cause." *The Kurdish Observer* 1 (Dec. 1987), pp. 8–9.

Kurdistan Popular Democratic Party (KPDP). "On the Deportation of Iraqi Kurds from Iraq." Apr. 7, 1982.

Mirkhan, H. "How Southern Kurdistan Became Part of Iraq." *Kurdistan Times* No. 1 (Winter 1990), pp. 123–29.

Morad, A. "The Wider Implications of Iraq's Use of Chemical Weapons Against Kurdish Targets." *The Kurdish Observer* No. 5 (Dec. 1988), pp. 13–14.

O'Connell, Patrick. "Genocide in Kurdistan." *Azadi Kurdistan* (South San Francisco, CA), Feb. 1991, pp. 1, 3.

Saeedpour, Vera Beaudin. "Insidious Intent: The Destruction and Depopulation of Iraqi Kurdistan." Briefing paper presented to the United States Congressional Human Rights Caucus, Oct. 20, 1989.

———. "Kurdish Times and the New York Times." *Kurdish Times* 2 (Summer 1988), pp. 25–41.

———. "From the Lion to the Fox: Iraqi Kurdish Refugees in Turkey." *Kurdish Times* 3 (Fall 1990), pp. 17–23.

Siaband, Samande [Izady, Mehrdad]. "Mountains, My Home: An Analysis of the Kurdish Psychological Landscape." *Kurdish Times* 2 (Summer 1988), pp. 7–11.

Simko, N. "Kurdistan—the Homeland of the Kurds." *Kurdistan Times* No. 1 (Winter 1990), pp. 66–89.

NEWSPAPERS AND MAGAZINES
Dailies

Christian Science Monitor, 1980–.
Financial Times, 1986–.
Guardian (London), 1986–.
Independent (London), 1986–.

International Herald Tribune, –.
Jerusalem Post, 1986–.
New York Times, 1974–.
Tennessean, 1986–.
Times (London), 1986–.
Wall Street Journal, 1986–.
Washington Post, 1972–.
Washington Times, 1986–.

WEEKLIES
Armenian Mirror–Spectator, 1987–.
Armenian Reporter, 1983–.
Armenian Weekly, 1983–.
Briefing (Turkey), 1984–.
Economist, 1983–.
Insight, 1987–.
Sunday Times (London), 1986–.
Time, 1986–.
Turkish Times, 1990–.

ARTICLES IN POPULAR JOURNALS

Bradshaw, David. "After the War: The Kurds." *World Today,* May 1991, pp. 78–80.

"The CIA Report the President Doesn't Want You to Read." [Pike Committee Report]. *The Village Voice,* Feb. 16, 1976, pp. 70–92. The part dealing with the Kurds is on pp. 85 and 87–88, and subtitled "Case 2: Arms Support."

Dinsmore, Lee. "The Forgotten Kurds." *The Progressive,* Apr. 1977, pp. 38–39.

Kaplan, Robert. "Iraqi Indigestion: Why Saddam Finds the Kurds Hard to Swallow." *The New Republic,* Oct. 8, 1990, pp. 14–15.

———. "Kurdistan: Sons of Devils." *The Atlantic,* Nov. 1987, pp. 38–44.

Kelly, Michael. "Back to the Hills." *The New Republic,* June 3, 1991, pp. 23–26.

Khalil, Samir al–. "Iraq and Its Future." *The New York Review of Books,* Apr. 11, 1991, pp. 10–14.

MacDonald, Scott B. "The Kurds in the 1990s." *Middle East Insight,* Jan.–Feb. 1990, pp. 29–35.

Makiya, Kanan. "The Anfal: Uncovering an Iraqi Campaign to Exterminate the Kurds." *Harper's* Magazine, May 1992, pp. 53–61.

Massing, Michael. "Can Saddam Survive?" *The New York Review of Books,* Aug. 15, 1991, pp. 59–64.

Mortimer, Edward. "Iraq: The Road Not Taken." *The New York Review of Books,* May 16, 1991, pp. 3–7.

SCHOLARLY PAPERS

Baker, Chahin. "Human Rights and the Kurds." Paper delivered at the Seminars organized by the Queensland Branch of Amnesty International, Griffith University, Aug. 6, 1989; and Queensland University, Aug. 7, 1989, Australia.

Frelick, Bill. "Kurdish Refugees and the New World Order." Paper delivered to the annual meeting of the Middle East Studies Association of North America, Washington, D.C., Nov. 25, 1991.

Izady, Mehrdad. "The Kurdish Demographic Revolution and the Future of the Middle East." Paper delivered to the annual meeting of the Middle East Studies Association of North America, Washington, D.C., Nov. 25, 1991.

Korn, David A. "The Kurds of Iraq Since the End of the Iran–Iraq War." Paper delivered to the annual meeting of the Middle East Studies Association of North America, Washington, D.C., Nov. 25, 1991.

Sheikmous, Omar. "The Current Situation of the Kurds in Iraq." Unpublished paper, June 1988.

———. "The Kurds in Exile." Paper delivered to the second annual meeting of the Kurdish Academy, Bremen, West Germany, June 18–19, 1988.

———. "The Kurds in the Iraq–Iran War and Since." Paper delivered to the International Colloquium on Ethnicity and Inter–state Relations in the Middle East, Berlin, West Germany, Apr. 20–23, 1989.

ARTICLES IN SCHOLARLY JOURNALS

Beck, Peter J. "A Tedious and Perilous Controversy: Britain and the Settlement of the Mosul Dispute, 1918–1926." *Middle Eastern Studies* 17 (April 1981), pp. 256–76.

Bolukbasi, Suha. "Turkey Copes with Revolutionary Iran." *Journal of South Asian and Middle Eastern Studies* 13 (Fall/Winter 1989), pp. 94–109.

Borovali, Ali–Fuat. "Kurdish Insurgencies, the Gulf War, and Turkey's Changing Role." *Conflict Quarterly* 7 (Fall 1987), pp. 29–45.

Bruinessen, Martin van. "Between Guerrilla War and Political Murder: The Workers' Party of Kurdistan." *Middle East Report* no. 153 (July–Aug. 1988), pp. 40–42, 44–46, 50.

———. "The Kurds between Iran and Iraq." *Middle East Report* no. 141 (July–Aug. 1986), pp. 14–27.

Edmonds, C. J. "Kurdish Nationalism." *Journal of Contemporary History* 6 (1971), pp. 87–107.

———. "The Kurds and the Revolution in Iraq." *The Middle East Journal* 13 (Winter 1959), pp. 1–10.

———. "The Kurds of Iraq." *The Middle East Journal* 11 (Winter 1957), pp. 52–62.

Entessar, Nader. "The Kurdish Mosaic of Discord." *Third World Quarterly* 11 (Oct. 1989), pp. 83–100.

———. "Kurdish Identity in the Middle East." *Current World Leaders* 34 (April 1991), pp. 270–82.

———. "The Kurds in Post–revolutionary Iran and Iraq." *Third World Quarterly* 6 (Oct. 1984), pp. 911–33.

Gunter, Michael M. "Kurdish Militancy in Turkey: The Case of PKK." *Crossroads*, no. 29 (1989), pp. 43–59.

———. "The Kurdish Insurgency in Turkey." *Journal of South Asian and Middle Eastern Studies* 13 (Summer 1990), pp. 57–81.

———. "The Kurdish Problem in Turkey." *The Middle East Journal* 42 (Summer 1988), pp. 389–406.

———. "Transnational Sources of Support for the Kurdish Insurgency in Turkey." *Conflict Quarterly* 11 (Spring 1991), pp. 7–29.

Harris, George S. "Ethnic Conflict and the Kurds." *Annals of the American Academy of Political and Social Science,* no. 433 (Sept. 1977), pp. 112–24.

Korn, David A. "Iraq's Kurds: Why Two Million Fled." *Foreign Service Journal.* 68 (July 1991), pp. 20–24.

MacDonald, Charles G. "The Impact of the Gulf War on the Iraqi and Iranian Kurds." *Middle East Contemporary Survey* 7 (1982–83), pp. 261–72.

———. "The Kurdish Challenge and Revolutionary Iran." *Journal of South Asian and Middle Eastern Studies* 13 (Fall/Winter 1989), pp. 52–68.

———. "The Kurds." *Journal of Political Science* 19 (1991), pp. 121–39.

Malek, Mohammed H. "Kurdistan in the Middle East Conflict." *New Left Review,* no. 175 (1989), pp. 79–94.

"Minorities in the Gulf War." *Cultural Survival Quarterly* 11, no. 4 (1987), p. 29.

Naamani, Israel T. "The Kurdish Drive for Self–Determination." *The Middle East Journal* 20 (Summer 1966), pp. 279–95.

Roosevelt, Archie Jr. "The Kurdish Republic of Mahabad." *The Middle East Journal 1* (July 1947), pp. 247–69.

Schmidt, Dana Adams. "The Kurdish Insurgency." *Strategic Review* 2 (Summer 1974), pp. 51–58.

Torrey, Gordon. "The Baath Ideology and Practice." *The Middle East Journal* 23 (Autumn 1969), pp. 445–70.

Wenner, Lettie M. "Arab–Kurdish Rivalries in Iraq." *The Middle East Journal* 17 (Winter/Spring 1963), pp. 68–82.

ARTICLES IN EDITED WORKS

Bois, Thomas, and Vladimir Minorsky. "Kurds, Kurdistan." *The Encyclopedia of Islam* (new edition), vol. 5, 1981, pp. 438–86.

Ghassemlou, A. R. "Kurdistan in Iran," in Gerard Chaliand, ed., *People without a Country: The Kurds and Kurdistan.* London: Zed Press, 1980, pp. 107–34.

Hazen, William E. "Minorities in Revolt: The Kurds of Iran, Iraq, Syria, and Turkey," in R. D. McLaurin, ed., *The Political Role of Minority Groups in the Middle East.* New York: Praeger, 1979, pp. 49–75.

Jawad, Sa'ad N. "The Kurdish Problem in Iraq," in Abbas Kelidar, ed., *The Integration of Modern Iraq.* London: Croom Helm, 1979, pp. 171–82.

———. "Recent Developments in the Kurdish Issue," in Tim Nibbock, ed., *Iraq: The Contemporary State* (New York: St. Martin's Press, 1982), pp. 47–61.

MacDonald, Charles G. "The Kurdish Question in the 1980s," in Milton J. Esman and Itamar Rabinovich, eds., *Ethnicity, Pluralism, and the State in the Middle East.* Ithaca: Cornell University Press, 1988, pp. 233–52.

"Memorandum of the Kurdish Rizgari Party, Baghdad, 18th January 1946," in F. David Andrews, ed., *The Lost Peoples of the Middle East: Documents of the Struggle for Survival and Independence of the Kurds, Assyrians, and Other Minority Races in the Middle East.* Salisbury: Documentary Publications, 1982, pp. 87–88.

Minorsky, Vladimir. "Kurdistan." *The Encyclopaedia of Islam,* 1927, pp. 1130–32.

———. "Kurds." *The Encyclopaedia of Islam,* 1927, pp. 1132–55.

[Nezan], Kendal. "Kurdistan in Turkey," in Gerard Chaliand, ed., *People without a Country: The Kurds and Kurdistan.* London: Zed Press, 1980, pp. 47–106.

———. "The Kurds under the Ottoman Empire," in Gerard Chaliand, ed., *People without a Country: The Kurds and Kurdistan.* London: Zed Press, 1980, pp. 19–46.

Shirkara, Ahmad A. R. "Prospects for Peace In Iraq: The Case of the Kurds and the Question of National Integration," in Charles Davies, ed., *After the War: Iran, Iraq and the Arab Gulf.* Chichester: Cardern Publications Ltd., 1990, pp. 97–114.

Vanly, Ismet Sheriff. "Kurdistan in Iraq," in Gerard Chaliand, ed., *People without a Country: The Kurds and Kurdistan.* London: Zed Press, 1980, pp. 153–210.

Viotti, Paul R. "Kurdish Insurgency in Iraq," in Bard E. O'Neill, D. J. Alberts, and Stephen J. Rossetti, eds., *Political Violence and Insurgency: A Comparative Approach.* Arvada, CO: Phoenix Press, 1974, pp. 327–57.

———. "Iraq: The Kurdish Rebellion," in Bard E. O'Neill, William R. Heaton, and Donald J. Alberts, eds., *Insurgency in the Modern World.* Boulder, CO: Westview Press, 1980, pp. 191–212.

Yapp, Malcolm. "'The Mice Will Play': Kurds, Turks and the Gulf War," in Hanns W. Maull and Otto Pick, eds., *The Gulf War: Regional and International Dimensions.* New York: St. Martin's Press, 1989, pp. 103–118.

Zubaida, Sami. "Community, Class and Minorities in Iraqi Politics," in Robert A. Fernea and William Roger Louis, eds., *The Iraqi Revolution of 1958: The Old Social Classes Revisited* (London: I. B. Tauris & Co. Ltd., 1991), pp. 197–210.

BOOKLETS

Hyman, Anthony. *Elusive Kurdistan: The Struggle for Recognition.* no. 214. London: The Centre for Security and Conflict Studies, 1988.

McDowall, David. *The Kurds.* no. 23. London: Minority Rights Group Ltd., 1985.

Pelletiere, Stephen C. *The Kurds and Their Agas: An Assessment of the Situation in Northern Iraq.* Carlisle Barracks, PA: Strategic Studies Institute, 1991.

Short, Martin, and Anthony McDermutt. *The Kurds.* no. 23. London: Minority Rights Group Ltd., 1975.

Sims, Richard. *Kurdistan: The Search for Recognition.* no. 124. London: The Institute for the Study of Conflict, 1980.

BOOKS

Abdulghani, J. M. *Iran & Iraq: The Years of Crisis.* London: Croom Helm, 1984.

Abu Jaber, Kamel S. *The Arab Ba'th Socialist Party: History, Ideology, and Organization.* Syracuse: Syracuse University Press, 1966.

Adams, Valerie. *Chemical Warfare, Chemical Disarmament.* Bloomington: Indiana University Press, 1990.

Adamson, David. *The Kurdish War.* New York: Praeger, 1965.

Arfa, Hassan. *The Kurds: An Historical and Political Study.* London: Oxford University Press, 1966.

Arif, Ismail al–. *Iraq Reborn: A Firsthand Account of the July 1958 Revolution and After.* New York: Vantage Press, 1982.

Barth, Fredrik. *Principles of Social Organization in Southern Kurdistan.* Oslo: Brodrene Jorgensen Boktrykkeri, 1953.

Batatu, Hanna. *The Old Social Classes and the Revolutionary Movements of Iraq: A Study of Iraq's Old Landed and Commercial Classes and of Its Communists, Ba'thists, and Free Officers.* Princeton, NJ: Princeton University Press, 1978.

Blau, Joyce. *Le probleme Kurde: Essai sociologique et historique.* Brussels: Centre pour l'Etude des Problemes du Monde Musulman Contemporain, 1963.

Black, Ian, and Benny Morris. *Israel's Secret Wars: A History of Israel's Intelligence Services.* New York: Grove Weidenfeld, 1991.

Bois, Thomas. *The Kurds,* trans. M. W. M. Welland. Beirut: Khayats, 1965.

Bruinessen, M. M. van. *Agha, Shaikh and State: On the Social and Political Organization of Kurdistan.* Utrecht: University of Utrecht, 1978.

Chubin, Shahram, and Charles Tripp. *Iran and Iraq at War.* Boulder, CO: Westview Press, 1988.

Chubin, Shahram, and Sepehr Zabih. *The Foreign Relations of Iran: A Developing State in a Zone of Great–Power Conflict.* Berkeley: University of California Press, 1974.

Cockburn, Andrew, and Leslie Cockburn. *Dangerous Liaison: The Inside Story of the US–Israeli Covert Relationship.* New York: Harper Collins Publishers, 1991.

Cordesman, Anthony H., and Abraham R. Wagner. *The Lessons of Modern War.* Vol. 2: *The Iran–Iraq War.* Boulder, CO: Westview Press, 1990.

Dann, Uriel. *Iraq under Qassem: A Political History, 1958–1963.* New York: Praeger, 1969.

Devlin, John. *The Baath Party: A History from Its Origins to 1966.* Stanford, CA: Hoover Institution Press, 1976.

Driver, G. R. *Kurdistan and the Kurds.* Mount Carmel, Britain: G. S. I. Printing Section, [1919].

Eagleton, William, Jr. *An Introduction to Kurdish Rugs and Other Weavings.* Brooklyn: Interlink Books, 1988.

———. *The Kurdish Republic of 1946.* London: Oxford University Press, 1963.

Edmonds, C. J. *Kurds, Turks and Arabs: Politics, Travel and Research in North-Eastern Iraq, 1919–1925*. London: Oxford University Press, 1957.

Entessar, Nader. *Kurdish Ethnonationalism*. Boulder, CO: Lynne Rienner Publishers, 1992.

Francisse, Anne. *The Problems of Minorities in the Nation-Building Process: The Kurds, the Copts, the Berbers*. New York: Vantage Press, 1971.

Franz, Erhard. *Kurden und Kurdentum: Zeitgeschichte eines Volkes und seiner Nationalbewegungen*. Hamburg: Deutsches Orient–Institut, 1986.

Gavan, S. S. *Kurdistan: Divided Nation of the Middle East*. London: Lawrence and Wishart, 1958.

Ghareeb, Edmund. *The Kurdish Question in Iraq*. Syracuse, NY: Syracuse University Press, 1981.

Ghassemlou, Abdul Rahman. *Kurdistan and the Kurds*. Prague: Czechoslovak Academy of Sciences, 1965.

Gunter, Michael M. *The Kurds in Turkey: A Political Dilemma*. Boulder, CO: Westview Press, 1990.

Haji, Aziz el–. *L'Irak nouveau et le probleme kurde*. Paris: Khayat, 1977.

Hamilton, A. M. *Road through Kurdistan: The Narrative of an Engineer in Iraq*. London: Faber and Faber Ltd., 1947.

Helms, Christine Moss. Iraq: *Eastern Flank of the Arab World*. Washington: The Brookings Institution, 1984.

Hourani, Albert H. *Minorities in the Arab World*. London: Oxford University Press, 1947.

Ismael, Tareq Y. *Iraq and Iran: Roots of Conflict*. Syracuse, NY: Syracuse University Press, 1982.

Izady, Mehrdad. *The Kurds: A Concise Handbook*. Washington, D.C.: Crane Russak, 1992.

Jawad, Sa'ad. *Iraq and the Kurdish Question, 1958–1970*. London: Ithaca Press, 1981.

Kahn, Margaret. *Children of the Jinn: In Search of the Kurds and Their Country*. New York: Seaview Books, 1980.

Karsh, Efraim, and Inari Rautsi. *Saddam Hussein: A Political Biography.* New York: Free Press, 1991.

Khadduri, Majid. *The Gulf War: The Origin and Implications of the Iraq–Iran Conflict.* New York: Oxford University Press, 1988.

———. *Independent Iraq: A Study in Iraqi Politics from 1932 to 1958,* 2d ed. London: Oxford University Press, 1960.

———. *Republican Iraq: A Study in Iraqi Politics Since the Revolution of 1958.* London: Oxford University Press, 1969.

———. *Socialist Iraq: A Study in Iraqi Politics Since 1968.* Washington: Middle East Institute, 1978.

Khalil, Samir al–. *The Republic of Fear: The Politics of Modern Iraq.* Berkeley: University of California Press, 1989.

Kissinger, Henry. *White House Years.* Boston: Little, Brown and Company, 1979.

Kinnane, Derk. *The Kurds and Kurdistan.* London: Oxford University Press, 1964.

Kreyenbroek, Philip G., and Stefan Sperl, eds. *The Kurds: A Contemporary Overview.* London: Routledge, 1992.

Kutschera, Chris. *Le mouvement national kurde.* Paris: Flammarion, 1979.

Lazier, Sheri. *Into Kurdistan: Frontiers under Fire.* London: Zed Books Ltd., 1991.

Longrigg, Stephen Hemsley. *Iraq, 1900 to 1950: A Political, Social, and Economic History.* London: Oxford University Press, 1953.

Marr, Phebe. *The Modern History of Iraq.* Boulder, CO: Westview Press, 1985.

McDowall, David. *The Kurds: A Nation Denied.* London: Minority Rights Publications, 1992.

Metz, Helen Chapin, ed. *Iraq: A Country Study.* Washington: Government Printing Office, 1990.

Middle East Watch. *Human Rights in Iraq.* New Haven, CT: Yale University Press, 1990.

Miller, Judith, and Laurie Mylroie. *Saddam Hussein and the Crisis in the Gulf.* New York: Times Books, 1990.

More, Christiane. *Les Kurdes d'aujourdhui: Mouvement national et partis politiques.* Paris: L'Harmattan, 1984.

Nikitine, Basile. *Les Kurdes: Etude sociologique et historique.* Paris: Imprimerie Nationale, 1956.

Nisan, Mordechai. *Minorities in the Middle East.* Jefferson: McFarland, 1991.

O'Ballance, Edgar. *The Gulf War.* London: Brassey's Defence Publishers, 1988.

———. *The Kurdish Revolt: 1961–1970.* Hamden, CT: Archon Books, 1973.

Olson, Robert. *The Emergence of Kurdish Nationalism and the Sheikh Said Rebellion, 1880–1925.* Austin: University of Texas Press, 1989.

Pelletiere, Stephen. *The Kurds: An Unstable Element in the Gulf.* Boulder, CO: Westview Press, 1984.

Powers, Thomas. *The Man Who Kept the Secrets: Richard Helms & the CIA.* New York: Alfred A. Knopf, 1979.

Ramazani, Ruhollah. *The Persian Gulf: Iran's Role.* Charlottesville: University Press of Virginia, 1972.

Rambout, Lucien. *Les Kurdes et le droit.* Paris: Le Cerf, 1947.

Raviv, Dan, and Yossi Melman. *Every Spy a Prince: The Complete History of Israel's Intelligence Community.* Boston: Houghton Mifflin, 1990.

Safrastian, Arshak. *Kurds and Kurdistan.* London: Harvil Press Ltd., 1948.

Schmidt, Dana Adams. *Journey Among Brave Men.* Boston: Little, Brown and Co., 1964.

Sloane, E. B. *To Mesopotamia and Kurdistan in Disguise: With Historical Notices of the Kurdish Tribes and the Chaldeans of Kurdistan.* London: John Murray, 1926.

Sluglett, Marion, and Peter Sluglett. *Iraq Since 1958: From Revolution to Dictatorship.* New York: St. Martin's Press, 1987.

Sluglett, Peter. *Britain in Iraq: 1914–1932.* London: Ithaca Press, 1976.

Smolansky, Oles M., and Bettie M. Smolansky. *The U.S.S.R. and Iraq.* Durham, NC: Duke University Press, 1991.

Spiers, Edward M. *Chemical Weaponry: A Continuing Challenge.* New York: St. Martin's Press, 1989.

Sykes, Mark. *The Caliph's Last Heritage: A Short History of the Turkish Empire.* London: Macmillan and Co., Ltd., 1915.

Wilson, Sir Arnold T. *Mesopotamia 1917–1920: A Clash of Loyalties.* Oxford: Oxford University Press, 1931.

Index

You Begin w/ Wilsons Pt. 12
"Non Turks in Ottoman emp. to
  have "autonomous dev."
Then The Treaty of Sevres ([19]20)
  "local autonomy" even "INDepende

Brits + Iraquis

TALK ABOUT THE BARZANI
                    TRIBE
IN the early 1930's Mulla MUSTAFA
  emerged as The leader.
                    CANCER in 79

Iraq in 1960 "Mulla is a freebooter
(Died in 79!) "he is The whole problem"

The 1970 MAnifesto | SADDAM Tried to
                   | "hit" B's son Idris

Mulla on The KDP "No Party. only The

TALK ABOut FOREIGN INfluences of
          ① USSR ② US ③ Israel

The Iran-Iraq war.
  chemical war - Kurds exhaust

The 91 Gulf war. US failed
Finally UN moving "Some"